The Caribbean Economies:

Perspectives on Social, Political and Economic Conditions

Edited by
Vincent R. McDonald
Howard University

MSS Information Corporation
655 Madison Avenue, New York, N.Y. 10021

This is a custom-made book of readings prepared
for the courses taught by the editor. For information about our program, please write to:

MSS INFORMATION CORPORATION
655 Madison Avenue
New York, New York 10021

MSS wishes to express its appreciation to the
authors of the articles in this collection for
their cooperation in making their work available
in this format.

Library of Congress Cataloging in Publication Data

McDonald, Vincent R   comp.
   The Caribbean economies.

   1. Caribbean area--Economic conditions. 2. Carib-
bean area--Social conditions. 3. Caribbean area--
Politics. I. Title.
HC155.M32   309.1'182'1   72-8622
ISBN 0-8422-5066-2
ISBN 0-8422-0258-7 (pbk.)

LCC Number 72-8622

PREFACE

The Caribbean represents an area of growing world focus as its emergence from direct political colonization to one moving towards economic domination has brought forward a spirit of nationalism and introspection demanding response.

As one moves from the larger former commonwealth countries which have recently shed their mantles of British rule to join the independent countries of the region one observes that the interests of academia, government and private enterprise are all seeking to more fully appreciate and understand not only the economic heritage but also the direction of their progress.

It is as a simple step on this journey that this book of readings is being offered. Its primary and most immediate use is to meet the needs of a course designed to investigate various problem areas associated with Caribbean growth and development.

Furthermore the articles are intended to be used by teachers and students in courses centered on the Caribbean in the areas of economic development, political science, sociology and contemporary issues. The materials may also be read independently or used as a frame of reference for related discussions.

Although space is a constraint, an attempt has been made to offer a cross-section of papers inclusive of the most pressing in the region. C.L.R. James's "Parties, Politics and Economics in the Caribbean" examines the political climate. The significance of Roy Preiswerk's concern with the "Relevance of Latin America to the Foreign Policy of Caribbean States" is seen when the paper on "Foreign Trade and Trade Policy of the English-speaking Caribbean States" is examined.

The problem of Economic Integration discussed by Brewster and McDonald should be seen in the context of the problems of planning as presented by Beckford and Waterston. Likewise, that of leadership and identity as discussed by Gomes, Frucht and Lotan is influential in discerning concerns of the level of Investment and the use and control of Resources offered by McIntyre, McDonald and Girvan.

The editor wishes to thank all the authors for their permission to use the selections that comprise the book. Naturally, I accept all criticisms regarding the selections and will welcome these or any suggestions for future works.

Vincent R. McDonald
Howard University

CONTENTS

1002565

TABLE 1

Proportion of Total Area in Farms by Size Group and Territory

(Percent)

Year	Territory	Size Group (acres)					
		< 5	5 < 25	25 - < 100	100 - < 500	500+	Total
--	Belize	n.a.	n.a.	n.a.	n.a.	n.a.	n.a.
1961	Barbados	13.4	2.4	2.5	50.4	31.3	100
1961	British Virgin Islands	5.7	43.7	34.2	16.4	--	100
--	Guyana	n.a.	n.a.	n.a.	n.a.	n.a.	n.a.
1968	Jamaica	14.9	22.1	8.3	9.9	44.9	100
	Leeward Islands						
1961	Antigua/Barbuda	26.7	9.7	4.4	17.1	42.2	100
--	Montserrat	n.a.	n.a.	n.a.	n.a.	n.a.	n.a.
1961	St. Kitts/Nevis/Anguilla	15.0	5.2	4.3	18.9	56.6	100
1963	Trinidad & Tobago*	6.9	30.7	15.1	16.2	31.1	100
	Windward Islands						
1961	Grenada	23.9	19.7	10.3	31.1	15.0	100
1961	Dominica	13.2	21.0	12.2	21.3	32.2	100
1961	St. Lucia	18.0	19.6	1.2	17.9	33.8	100
1961	St. Vincent	27.0	24.5	7.69	16.0	24.2	100

*Provisional Estimates for holdings of one acre and over (excluding land owned by Government)

Source: Department of Agricultural Economics, Some Agricultural Statistics of the Commonwealth Caribbean, St. Augustine, Trinidad, 1972.

of choices for policy makers but in spite of
the similarities, there is enough uniqueness
on the part of the respective countries which
demands that its program be viewed in the
context of its own set of conditions. Given
the existence of variations, a systematic
study of these variations and their consequences will be helpful in evaluating the
linkages between reform programs, income
distribution and employment effects.

Land reform[3] as usually viewed implies
principally a coercive redistribution of
ownership or operative rights to land, and
can be divided into three main sub-areas:
(1) expropriation of the land in favor of
new owners, (2) payment of compensation,
if any, and (3) financing the compensation
or other costs of the land reform.[4] Reform
could take an entire property, or could take
only a part if some of the land was being
put to the intended use.

The need for some level of reform
among the countries of this region can be

---

[3]Dorothy Warriner defines it as "The
redistribution of property in land for the
benefit of small farmers and agricultural
workers." "Land Reform and Economic Development," Agriculture in Economic Development,
ed. Carl K. Eicher and Lawrence W. Witt,
(New York, McGraw Hill Book Co.).

[4]Scott M. Eddie. "The Simple Eco-
nomics of Land Reform: The Expropriation-
Compensation Process and Income Distribution"
(Madison, Wisconsin, The Land Tenure Center,
February, 1971), p. 1.

of the development in this area has resulted
from a systematic process of exploitation--
of land, mineral resources, and more important people. There exists inequalities in
resource ownership and income distribution
with all the concomitant social ills which
follow. (Low levels of literacy, skills,
social development, etc.).

Statistics of the region reveal that
an average of 40 percent of the labor force
is engaged in agricultural activities and 50
percent of the land area (55 percent if
Guyana is excluded) is in farm lands.

With farm land concentrated in the
hands of relatively few large owners the
average man does not share significantly in
the decisions or incomes derived from the
agricultural sector. A typical example of
this would be the situation in Barbados
where land in farms is estimated at over 70
percent of total land area. However, during
the 1960's, the Ministry of Agriculture,
estimated that only 12,000 acres or approximately 23 percent of farm land was owned by
peasants.[5]

In any system where a large proportion of the population is engaged in agriculture (20-53 percent or more) a system of
agriculture which retards incentive and production acts as a deterrance to economic
advance. It is only as the productivity in
agriculture increases that expansions can be
expected in other sectors.

---

[5]Economic Planning Unit, _Barbados
Economic Survey_, 1968, p. 32.

The need for land reform and a process of income distribution is neither unique nor relegated to the so-called developing countries. A historical review would point up the fact that the developed countries faced this problem within the past two centuries.[6] In fact, it might be argued that these problems are still being faced. More recently, the Middle and Far East, Eastern Europe, Latin America and our own Caribbean countries have all been making attempts to confront and meet this problem.

These countries have faced the same perplexing questions: What is the existing distribution of land, income and other agricultural resources? What is the impact of the existing distribution on the economy? Would a change in this pattern improve the distribution of wealth and the state of the economy? The solutions to these questions cannot be found solely within the context of

---

[6]In a report, Progress in Land Reform by the U.N. they summarized, "the replies received [from member countries] continue to reflect the wide contrasts between different countries in respect of institutions and economic conditions in agriculture and in the consequent need for reform. The relevant policies adopted in the economically advanced countries have as their objective improvement of the institutional framework of agriculture, without major changes in the agrarian structure. In the less developed countries, the importance of a sound tenure system is increasingly recognized as a precondition for development of agriculture and other sectors of the economy."

economics. For a wide variety of reasons
they revolve around different institutional
problems of land tenure, differing social,
political as well as geographic considerations.

The implementation of a program of
reform causes concern in deciding what
standards must receive priority. Warriner,
for example, points out, "there often appears
to be conflict between the demand for greater
social equality and the need for increasing
efficiency in agriculture. The kind of
society we should like to live in is not
necessarily the kind of economy that will
feed us best. Which should be the standard
social justice or economic efficiency?[7] This
is a question which must be faced within
these countries.

The pros and cons of the possible
impact of a program of land reform upon the
level of employment in the agricultural
sector is an important one in the instituting
of any program.

I have seen various commentaries by
government and public media over the past
several years on the level of employment in
the various Caribbean countries. What is
alarming is that these estimates of 12-20
percent[8] of unemployment has become so common
that no great alarm appears to be exhibited
at its mention. Perhaps of greater concern

---

[7]Warriner, p. 273.

[8]Commonwealth Caribbean Regional
Secretariat, CARIFTA, The New Caribbean.

is the fact that there appears to be no common technique being applied in measuring unemployment and underemployment including the natural and regional distributions, consequently programs supposedly geared towards increasing employment are often implemented without a clear notion as to the extent of the problem.

The resulting inequalities in the control of resources and the disparity in income distribution, the low level of relevant education and skills; and social development of the entire population all lend credence to the conclusion that some form of change must be instituted. The bulk of the people in this region is engaged in producing goods which are not for their own consumption, and which provides little benefits to the country in general.[9] They have been tools of exploitation and colonization.

While the exploitation of the resources of this region is a common phenomenon among developing countries (and even in many so-called developed countries) it is necessary that of a minimum the returns from such exploitation should find its way back into the economy to spur the "other sectors" if a modicum of growth and hopefully development is to be achieved.

----

[9]"While export agriculture remains in this vulnerable portion, the domestic agricultural sector (producing food and livestock products for the local and regional markets) is in a very undeveloped state; and this results in very high and growing levels of imports of food from the outside world." CARIFTA, p. 10.

Programs geared towards the retention or recycling of profits from such activities should therefore be developed and encouraged by Government.

Basis for Reform

What is paramount here is that a program of land reform involves obstensibly a direct public action to rearrange the ownership and use of land with a view towards the scattering of large holding (and/or the consolidation of already small units) and the ultimate spreading of wealth and income.

Such a conclusion is in keeping with the Economic & Social Council of the U.N. who in Resolution 1078 of July 28, 1965, calls for governments to "take measures for rapid implementation of land reform in the interest of landless and small peasants and agricultural hired laborers." They went on to add that "the land will become, for the man who tills it, the basis of his economic and social welfare."[10] In that conference the following emerged as the more important ways in which a variety of countries were meeting the problem of reform:

(a) Transfer to cultivating tenants of the ownership of the land they cultivate;

(b) Transfer between operative units, reducing larger farms and expanding small ones;

---

[10] United Nations, Report of the World Land Reform Conference (Rome, Italy, 20 June - 2 July, 1966), p. 7.

(c)   Creating new farms by breaking up large estates;

(d)   Conversion of large farms into workers' co-operatives;

(e)   Profit-sharing farms (as in Puerto Rico);

(f)   Nationalization of land and its distribution among peasants in individual holdings or in co-operatives;

(g)   Establishment of state farms on the alienated large estates of big landowners or the establishment of "peoples' farms," as in Cuba, on the expropriated land of foreign or local plantations or latifundia;

(h)   The transfer of abandoned large estates belonging to former Colonial Power to peasants without land in some such system as autogestion, as in Algeria.[11]

It is obvious that reform is not merely the redistribution of land. It embraces a restructuring of the existing pattern of tenure arrangements, conditions of settlement, credit arrangements and tax policies.

_____

[11]U.N., p. 7.

16

In addition, it necessitates the institution of a set of policies geared towards
the absorption of larger segments of the agricultural population in tenured positions of
the farms capable of improving the status of
agricultural production to meet the needs of
the entire country.

As previously indicated, the nature
of the program of reform needed for a given
country or region by necessity will depend on
a number of considerations. In fact, the
needed changes may evolve from the history of
the country.

For those in and outside of the
region steeped in the niceties of the sanc-
tity of the institution of private property,
freedom of choice, and competition the mere
mention of the term "land reform" conjures
up a feeling of uncertainty and pending revolution. These feelings, whether real or
imagined, are caused by a misunderstanding
of what land reform really means. While
Reform does appear to violate the institutions mentioned, the nature of the origin of
ownership, the exploitative use of land on
the one hand and the non or inefficient use
on the other, all point to the need to free
land for its best use.[12] Action taken to
adjust historical inequities becomes a
mandatory function of government as representatives of the people. Distributive and

---

[12]This becomes a matter of weighing
the costs and benefits associated with the
acquisition and reassignment of the
property.

equalizing reforms are not inconsistent with the aspirations of the people of developing countries. In order to improve the status of the people, changes in the following areas are prerequisites: The form of land ownership, opportunities to obtain skills necessary to share in the wealth of the country and access to employment opportunities. A reluctance to implement these changes can only lead to repudiation of policy makers. It is this concern which at various times has resulted in the introduction of programs of reform in a number of Latin American, Asian, African, and even European countries.[13]

In view of the complexity of a program of land reform and the range of choices which the various countries of the region face, the question must be raised as to what forms should a program of reform in this region take.

Bearing in mind the primary basis advanced for such a program I will itemize what a program should do and leave the specific implementation to those holding this responsibility.[14]

---

[13]For a discussion of these see for example, Land Reform in Developing Countries, ed. James R. Brown and Sein Lin; Agrarian Reform in Latin America, ed. T. Lynn Smith (N.Y. Alfred A. Knopf, 1965) and Elias H. Tuma, Twenty-six Centuries of Agrarian Reform: A Comparative Analysis, (University of Cal. Press, 1965).

[14]It should be recognized that some of these are in conflict with each other, of course.

Among the goals any land reform program in this region of the World should include are:

(a) Result in a redistribution of
underutilized or unused farmable
lands.

(b) Create a pattern of land use consistent with established National
priorities and needs.

(c) Reduce the imbalances of income
and wealth.

(d) Reduce the level of malnutrition
and improve the caloric contents
of the nation.

(e) Provide opportunities for ownership
over long term periods.

(f) Seek to reduce the dependence on
imported agricultural commodities.

(g) Improve the system of production
and marketing--collection and
dispersion--necessary to facilitate the success of the reforms.

(h) Provide a network of incentives
and facilitating services to encourage production over and above
personal needs.

(i) Establish a program of education
outside of the existing educational
institutions to meet the needs of
the "Reformed."

What this suggests then is that each
country or the region should institute an
immediate assessment of/or reassessment of
distribution and use of their land. A set
of priorities in use should be established
and some legal body be constituted to carry
out the dictates of that policy under terms
of reference such as those suggested above.

Impact on Employment and Income

The impact of a program of reform on
the level of employment and distribution of
incomes are probably the most important concerns of those involved in assessing the
policy implications of such programs.

It is true that while a program of
reform is likely to have considerable equity
benefit for the beneficiaries of such reforms
it is not correspondingly true that such a
reallocative process necessarily results in
the most efficiency. This depends on intent
of the reform--social or economic; and
whether the most competent farmers are
benefiting.

While studying small farming in
Jamaica, David Edwards for example points
out, "The possession of land and the amount
possessed are important determinants of
status in the small [Jamaican] farm communities. Other things being equal, the
landless agricultural worker has the lowest
status, next is the man with a small piece
of land who has to work for someone else a
great deal, then the man with enough land
not to have to work out much and employing

20

some labour, and finally the man with many acres of land who never has to work off his farm and who employs a considerable amount of labor."[15]

While the objectives of a program of reform is likely to vary, the primary impact is often more political rather than social. Politically the reformer is likely to ingrain himself with larger segments of the population than those who he offends. Hopefully, there is some level of social and economic changes resulting from the process of reallocation in the form of aided income and increased employment. It is noted, however that in general the relative social status between the losers and receivers of land does not change, thus a dilemma. The countries need growth in the agricultural sector if they are to sever the chains of poverty, but they also need social justice as well, both for humanitarian reasons and also for ultimate political and social stability.[16]

In the Caribbean, throughout South America, in Southeast Asia, in Ceylon and in parts of East Africa, the agrarian structure is dominated by large estates.[17]

---

[15]David Edwards, An Economic Study of Small Farming in Jamaica (I.S.E.R., 1961), p. 77.

[16]Blinkhorn, p. 22.

[17]United Nations, "Land Reform: Defects in Agrarian Structure and Obstacles to Economic Development," Development and Society: The Dynamics of Economic Change, ed. David E. Novack (New York, St. Martin's Press, 1964), p. 118.

These plantations are large, centrally directed establishments employing paid labor. This form of operation which generally operates quite efficiently thrives on conditions in which crop production is geared primarily towards exports making use of the surplus of labor.

In the presence of such a system, it is questionable whether a program of reform based on the acquisition and fragmentation (into economical unit sizes) of such plantations would substantially improve aggregate employment. In the situation where we assume that the reform is based on cultivated "plantation" land, e.g., sugar cane land, the primary need for change is social.[18] Further, it is not irrational

---

[18]A U.N. paper for example points out that, "Since the need for maintaining employment must be a paramount consideration in these overcrowded islands [Caribbean], whatever new forms of organization are created must aim at promoting intensive use of the land. It is generally believed that the division of the plantations into small farms would be likely to reduce the area planted to sugar-cane, which would reduce the demand for labor and also the volume of agricultural production. So far as plantation crops other than sugar are concerned, the difference in yields between large and small farms is not great enough to outweigh the social advantages which would be gained by resettlement on smaller farms." (Ibid., p. 121).

to assume that it might very well be that the existing acreage of such plantations are in excess of that desirable for the firm (plantation) to operate at its optimum level.

C. Y. Thomas, in a study of the Guyana Sugar Industry for example, points an accusing finger at the industry as he points out:

> The evidence of an in-built dynamic towards increasing exploitation is abundantly clear. The industry makes large and rapid expansions in its utilized acreage and output; it pays substantial dividend rates, it raises no new capital abroad; at the same time it uses absolutely less labour; it pays absolutely less taxes and its investment rate is below the average size of the sector.[19]

A reallocation of ownership of such land into the hands of small farmers assisted with all the facilitating services at a National level could well maintain if not surpass the level of employment and production and unquestionably result in an added flow of income within the country. This income is a potential source of additional

---

[19]Clive Thomas, "Sugar Economics in a Colonial Situation: A Study of the Guyana Sugar Industry," Ratoon, Studies in Exploitation, No. 1.

taxable income which naturally provides
linkages with the rest of the economy--i.e.,
the sector could make additional contributions to public receipts and indirectly
result in increased employment.

Additionally, as each country assesses
the implication of external market forces,
e.g., Britain's entry into the E.C.M. it
might well find that alternative crops will
have to be grown if it is not to be left
holding "the bag." Without attempting to
minimize the importance of sugar to the
economy of most Caribbean countries it must
be pointed out that the net contribution of
this sector must be considered in relation
to the opportunity cost of producing those
commodities that would reduce the extent of
foreign exchange spent importing food.

In those instances where the government is desirous of changing the existing
relationships with its large foreign land
owners without engaging in a program of
reform (expropriation or confiscation) it
might well legislate minimum wages and
standards of employment along with a policy
of taxation geared towards ensuring that an
equitable share of earned profits remain
and is recycled within the country. The
imposition of such a policy should have a
positive employment effect in both the long
and short run.

The other large blocs of land available for possible reform programs are Government or "Crown" lands. While we cannot
correlate land reform with attempts either
to reclaim unproductive land or to settle
farmers in formerly uninhabited areas, it
can be readily seen that the introduction

of land which up to that time was not in use will
make positive contributions to income and employment and hence to the level of living of the
people.

Conclusion

The introduction of a program of land
reform by Caribbean countries could be an important step in improving the contributions of
the agricultural sector to economic development.

Land reform involves the adoption of a
new pattern of income distribution. The technique of acquisition of the land is important:
If the land is purchased rather than expropriated then the impact is similar to a real
estate transaction. If the land is paid for
in bonds, then the government is in effect
receiving a loan equivalent to the price of
the land. To be effective then, land reform
involves taking productive land (hence income)
from existing owners without immediate compensation otherwise there is no redistributive
and hence little employment effects.

In conclusion the rationale for the
program may be summarized as:

(a)　It provides a redistribution of
income;

(b)　It provides increased social and
economic benefits;

(c)　It serves as a basis of increased
employment depending on the nature
of land being distributed;

(d)　It provides additional revenue for
government in the form of tax
revenue.

REFERENCES

Blinkhorn, Thomas A. "People of the Land,"
International Bank for Reconstruction
and Development, Washington, D.C., 1972.

Brewster, Havelock and Thomas Clive. The
Dynamics of West Indian Economic Inte-
gration. (Institute of Social and
Economic Research, V.W.I., 1967).

Brown, James R. and Linn, Sein, ed. Land
Reform in Developing Countries, 1967
International Seminar on Land Taxation,
Land Tenure, and Land Reform in Develop-
ing Countries, Taiwan, 1967.

Dorner, Peter and Felstehausen, Herman.
Agrarian Reform and Employment: The
Colombian Care. (Land Tenure Center,
The University of Wisconsin, Madison,
Wisconsin, 53 706.)

Eddie, Scott M. "The Simple Economics of
Land Reform." The Land Tenure Center,
No. 75, Madison, Wisconsin, February,
1971.

Edwards, David. An Economic Study of Small
Farming in Jamaica, Institute of
Social and Economic Research, V.W.I.,
1961.

Eicher, Carl K. and Witt, Lawrence W. ed.
Agriculture in Economic Development.
(New York, McGraw-Hill Book Co., 1964).

Maddison, Angus. Economic Progress and
Policy in Developing Countries. New
York, W. W. Norton & Company, Inc.,
1970.

Novack, David E. and Lekaehman, Robert, ed.
    Development and Society, _The Dynamics
    of Economic Change_ (New York, St.
    Martin's Press, 1964).

Smith, T. Lynn, ed., _Agrarian Reform in
    Latin America_. (New York, Alfred A.
    Knopf, 1965).

Thomas, Clive. "Sugar Economics in a
    Colonial Situation: A Study of the
    Guyana Industry," _Ratoon, Studies in
    Exploitation_, No. 1.

Tuma, Elias H. _Twenty-six Centuries of
    Agrarian Reform: A Comparative Analysis_,
    University of California Press, 1965.

United Nations, _Report of the World Land
    Reform Conference_, Rome, Italy, 1966.

Palmier, L. H. _Organization of Land
    Redistribution Beneficiaries_, UNRISD
    Report No. 70.1, Geneva, 1970.

PARTIES, POLITICS AND ECONOMICS IN THE CARIBBEAN

C. L. R. JAMES

To THINK CORRECTLY and fruitfully of parties and politics in the West Indies demands that the politics and the parties be seen within the context of an affinity which exists and must be borne in mind in every estimate of their future.

Any survey of the kind must take warning from the example of two great sons of the Caribbean, Marcus Garvey and George Padmore, and one American thinker, W. E. B. Du Bois. Twenty-five years ago, different, even antagonistic, as their individual opinions and activities might have been, they saw and therefore worked for an Africa that was far closer to the reality than the Africa that was being administered by authoritative officials and analyzed by learned pundits and travelers of the day. The Africa of today did not fall from the sky. Below the superficial surface, Garvey, Padmore and Du Bois saw the African reality. To see realistically (and charitably) the politics and parties of the West Indies requires an awareness of the underlying reality, a reality which is not too far below the surface.

There is an apparently bewildering variety of West Indian, or more strictly speaking, Caribbean politics and parties and governments. There is the vigorous and revolutionary government of Cuba, a focus of the world conflict which dominates our age, a focus also of the struggle of an underdeveloped country to achieve the concrete independence which it considers an indispensable requirement for its full development. There is only one party in Cuba and its political constitution and personalities and procedures are of a type familiar to all who have the most casual acquaintance with political parties striving to project a country from one stage into another. Just next door is the Puerto Rican government constitutionally dominated for many years by the political party headed by Muñoz Marin. Underlying its consistent adherence to democratic procedures and forms is an ambiguous relation with the government of the United States. Is it to become the fifty-first state or is it to continue as some

---

C. L. R. James was born in Trinidad in 1901. Most of his life he has been a socialist in the forefront of the fight against imperialism. Of his many books, the best known are "Black Jacobins" and "A History of Negro Revolt."

FREEDOMWAYS, Third Quarter, 1964, pp. 312-318.

28

sort of, as yet undefined, territory enjoying the double privileges of independence and the benevolent patronage of the United States? Muñoz Marin continues to exercise dominance while holding this vital question in abeyance for the simple reason that for the people of Puerto Rico the decision calls for an agonizing reappraisal which they are not ready to make. The basic reason is not far to seek and can be visualized in quite different territories. Jamaica and Trinidad and Tobago, two former British colonies in the Caribbean, have been granted independence and the Prime Minister of Trinidad, Dr. Eric Williams, has clarified the dilemma which is a ball and chain at the feet of all West Indian political parties and politicians. Feeling the strains hidden behind the freedom of a national flag and a national anthem, and in face of the Medusa-like visage of the British government which says, "OK. You are independent. *Be independent,* especially of my economic resources," the Prime Minister declared that Trinidad and Tobago found a closer affinity with Yugoslavia and Egypt than with the Britain which had ruled and guided it for 150 years. What has a Caribbean territory in common with Egypt of the Pyramids or of the Nile, with its native language, a religion and way of life thousands of years old? Yet this statement expressed an urgent reality, the abiding reality of all West Indian politics and parties.

What are they?

Who are they?

Where are they going?

They do not know, and their position is therefore a constant series of spurts, now to right and now to left, unpredictable by anyone because they themselves do not know (or will not see) where they are, and therefore cannot take two firm steps either forward or backward. The drift, however, is clear, towards reaction internally and a neo-colonialist relation with a Great Power, preferably the United States.

The political problem which faces Muñoz Marin was stated with his customary disregard for conventional opinion by General de Gaulle. Martinique and Guadeloupe are no longer French colonies. They have been made into departments of France and a few months ago were paid an official visit by the General. It certainly was not by accident that the General stated most brutally his response to the perennial West Indian problem. Africa, he said, could be decolonized because Africa had a native civilization and an African way of life. "But you West Indians," continued the General, "have nothing of the kind. *You are French";* and warming to his theme, he continued, "look at yourselves on the map, you are no more than dust."

Thus thrown back on their small and insignificant selves, not only by history but in their own consciousness, West Indian politics waver between the democracy of Muñoz Marin, Trinidad and Tobago and Jamaica, seeking a national identity; and the ferocity amounting not infrequently to savagery of the regimes of Duvalier in Haiti and the bandit Trujillo and his successors in the Dominican Republic.

It may seem strange and even extreme to encompass politics and parties so different as the politics of Fidel Castro, Juan Bosch (the successor of Trujillo, recently expelled from the Dominican Republic after winning an unquestioned majority in a democratic election), the apparently stable government of Muñoz Marin and the routine of constitutional elections that seem established in Jamaica and Trinidad. Yet the underlying identity is deeply rooted in the social and economic relations of centuries. Whatever the form of government, or the coloration of political parties, the permanent features of Caribbean society, dominating their politics, are three, three in one and one in three.

The whole population is expatriate. Slaves, freed slaves, former non-slaves, emigrants from India, economic masters, none is native in any admissible sense of that word. The languages, the pattern of life are European. Even where, as in British Guiana and Trinidad, there is a large East Indian population, they do not seek to return to their land of origin, they strive with notable success to master the Western language.

This potentially explosive population lives enclosed within what is accurately entitled: the old colonial system. Banks, agricultural estates, industries, newspapers, radio (now television), import and export forms, are 90 per cent in the hands of foreign firms or what are in essence their local representatives. In this respect 1964 is no different from 1664. Twice this iron framework has been broken through: in 1792-1804 Toussaint L'Ouverture and the slaves of French San Domingo got out of it by smashing the system completely. In 1958 Fidel Castro did the same. The crisis with which he struggles shows the tremendous break with the past, the whole past, which is involved. The degeneration of Haiti is an example not of Negro backwardness but of the consequences of a partial break out from the old colonial system.

The third constituent of the Caribbean trinity is the sugar plantation. That is and always has been the social basis of the Caribbean system.

That environment, a population of expatriates, trained and daily

30

educated in the existentialia of Western democracy and way of life; the total ownership and control of the nerve-centers of economic and social life by foreign economic and financial powers; the discipline into acceptance of the regime by the large mass of the population on sugar plantations, with here and there thousands of small peasants who eke out a precarious existence between their small plots of land and in crop-time going to work on the plantations.

To this day the West Indian Negro must be seen as a historically different social being from his brothers of the United States. In his seminal work, *The Masters and the Slaves*, Gilberto Freyre writes:

"The Brazilian Negro appears to us, throughout the whole of our colonial life and the first phase of our independent life as a nation, as a being deformed by slavery, by slavery and by the one-crop system, of which he was the instrument, the firm point of support, unlike the Indian, who was always on the move."

That is the general key to the history of the Negro people in the Americas. The particular West Indian variety is that the sugar plantation was the most striking example of the one-crop system and, *slavery or no slavery, continues to this day.*

A new and apparently indigestible element has been added to the centuries-old pattern. Companies, again foreign, have introduced the production of oil, bauxite and mine industries. The workers organized in these, freed from the demoralizing discipline of the sugar plantation, express the national resentment by continued strikes for higher wages, fringe benefits, the ill-manners of a superior, anything. It therefore becomes a function of government to reduce to colonial subordination this intrusion from a new age. All that the old colonial system can conceive is to fit modern labor into the old system —a very hard task.

This new system of independence is only the old colonial system writ large. Contemporary Caribbean politics consists essentially of the capacity to administer the old colonial system either by means of the brutality of a Trujillo or the democratic forms of Trinidad or Jamaica, or the skillful balancing on the fence of Muñoz Marin.

The Caribbean territories have a universal significance far beyond their size and social weight. They seem to be a slice of Western civilization put under a microscope for the scientific investigation of the fundamental predicates and perspectives of that civilization itself. Owing to the expatriate character of the whole Caribbean all the old problems seem posed anew in terms which are easily grasped, new in that they are not dominated as in the older countries by long-established growths and accretions; urgent in that the Caribbean problems demand some settlement if not solution; comprehensive and very modern in that politics, economics and sociology are one indivisible unit. Here are some startling and far-reaching examples.

1. Take the racial problem. The world is pained and even horrified by what is believed to be the indestructible racial antagonism between Negroes and East Indians in British Guiana, led on the one hand by the East Indian Dr. Jagan and on the other by the Negro Burnham. The truth of these apparently suicidal politics is that in 1952 Jagan and Burnham were joined together in one party—and were virtual masters of British Guiana, the races closer together than they were ever before, and showing every sign that they were eager for further integration. It seems to me that the racial antagonism in British Guiana is an effect, not a cause, the effect of the unwillingness or inability of some leaders there to challenge the old colonial system.

2. Mr. Manley of Jamaica, defeated by Sir Alexander Bustamante over federation and in the struggle for power, has recently made the public announcement that the similarity (hostile critics say identity) of the two rival parties in Jamaica is the condition of democracy and order. If the two parties, he declared, had fundamentally different ideas as to the kind of society they envisaged or aimed at, the democratic regime would be impossible. Mr. Manley is quite correct. Both parties intend not to interfere with the old colonial system. Whence a growing discontent, even anger, in all West Indian territories. In territory after territory it is the same. In political policy the Opposition parties are indistinguishable from the government party. Recently Dr. Williams, Prime Minister of Trinidad and Tobago, declared that 90 per cent of the economy is in the hands of two or three foreign firms. The leader of the Opposition, we may be sure, is thinking about it no less and no more than Dr. Williams.

3. After the assassination of Trujillo in the Dominican Republic Senor Juan Bosch was elected by a large majority. But he made no attempt to touch the old colonial system. He therefore aroused no popular enthusiasm and was easily ejected by the old gang.

4. Federation is on the order of the day and this is how the British West Indian Federation collapsed. The old colonial system consisted of insular economies, each with its financial and economic capital in London. A federation meant that the economic line of direction should no longer be from island to London, but from island to island. But that involved the break-up of the old colonial system. The West Indian politicians preferred the break-up of the Federation.

5. The French Caribbean territories find that becoming departments of France has doubly and trebly strengthened the old colonial system. It is the finished pattern of the French community in Africa and the Dutch community in South America.

6. Contrary to general belief, the West Indies are not sunk in irremediable poverty. There is room for only two proofs, each of such diverse origin that together they are irrefutable. The first is the American Government. In the *New York Times* of the 8th of October, 1962, appeared a report of Mr. Chester Bowles, appointed Special Adviser to President Kennedy on Underdeveloped Areas. Mr. Bowles divided recipients of American aid into three categories. In the first category Mr. Bowles places nations with a per capita gross national product of more than $350. Their current problems, the report stated, would be sufficiently acute to require aid, but their difficulties would result primarily from the "misuse and maldistribution of their wealth." In this category along with Greece, Venezuela and others we find Jamaica and Trinidad. He added that these countries should be able "to put their financial houses in order." In addition to corrective measures which the United States should suggest, they would be advised to introduce tax and land reforms.

That mishandling and maldistribution of resources is the direct continuation of the old colonial system.

The other critical view of the West Indian economy and West Indian society is that of Professor Arthur Lewis. When he was Principal of the University of the West Indies in Jamaica, Professor Lewis, former head of the faculty of economics at Manchester University and at the time of writing a member of the faculty at Princeton, tried to remove some cobwebs from the eyes of his fellow West Indians:

"This opinion that the West Indies can raise all the capital it needs from its own resources is bound to shock many people, because West Indians like to feel that ours is a poor community. But the fact of the matter is that at least half of the people in the world are poorer than we are. The standard of living in the West Indies is higher than the standard of living in India, or China, in most of the countries of Asia, and in most of the countries of Africa. The West Indies is not a poor community; it is in the upper bracket of world income. It is capable of producing the extra five or six per cent of resources which is required for this job, just as Ceylon and Ghana are finding the money they need for development by taxing themselves. It is not necessary for us to send our statesmen around the world begging for help. If help is given to us let us accept it, but let us not sit down and say nothing can be done until the rest of the world out of its goodness of heart is willing to grant us charity."

In other words the economic problem is soluble but as in far larger countries soluble only by political means. The question is: who will bell the cat?

The problem does not imperatively or inescapably demand revolutionary measures, e.g., violence such as took place in French San Domingo in 1791 or in Cuba in 1958. Many elements both at home and abroad recognize the explosive character of the Caribbean scene. The West Indian white is not a foreigner. He is a West Indian and many of them recognize that something must be done and can be done. That, however, is another story and involves the ways and means to a federation of the whole Caribbean area. That may sound utopian, as utopian as Garvey, Padmore and Du Bois must have sounded when they talked of an independent Africa.

Roy Preiswerk
Director, Institute of
  International Relations
University of the West Indies
St. Augustine, Trinidad, W.I.

THE RELEVANCE OF LATIN AMERICA TO THE FOREIGN POLICY OF COMMONWEALTH CARIBBEAN STATES[1]

For the leaders and people of every new state of Asia, Africa and the Caribbean, independence has brought about a dramatic awakening with respect to the conceptualization of their position in world affairs. The loosening of ties with the metropolis, which had been the primary aim of the struggle for independence, suddenly appears in a double perspective. On the one hand, it contains the threat of distintegration of the established social and economic order and, on the other hand, it opens prospects for new bonds and opportunities. After decades or centuries of predominantly bilateral relationships between colony and metropolis, historical links are confronted with the pressures resulting from geographic proximity.The diversification of foreign contacts is a phenomenon of the very recent past. The leaders and inhabitants of Ghana and the Ivory Coast, Nigeria and Niger, Trinidad and Venezuela, or Guyana and Brazil are only now realizing the full impact of their relationship as neighbours. To understand the shock which this process of regional familiarization creates in some situations, the analyst may still study the source of the difficulty of adjustment in a "live" situation. Indeed, the totality of colonial bilateralism, encompassing commercial, political, human, and spiritual relations, can be witnessed in such countries as Martinique or Angola where

---

[1] At the recent Heads of Government Conference the term "Commonwealth Caribbean" was officially accepted to designate the English-speaking territories regardless of constitutional status. "Commonwealth Caribbean States" consequently applies to Jamaica, Trinidad and Tobago, Barbados, and Guyana. The term "West Indies" shall be applied as consistently as possible to cover English-speaking Caribbean islands only, exclusive of Guyana and British Honduras.

JOURNAL OF INTER-AMERICAN STUDIES, 1969,
Vol. 11, No. 2, pp. 245-271.

the outlook of the elites continues to be exclusively oriented towards the metropolis in total ignorance of the Caribbean or African environment.

In the case of the new English-speaking Caribbean States, the development of regional and extra-regional links to compensate for the disintegration of the colonial relationship plays a particularly important role in the formulation of foreign policy. The peculiarity of the situation stems from the fact that the clash of historical and geographical determinants of foreign policy is exceptionally violent: here is a group of Commonwealth countries, appearing on the world scene as small, separate units, with constitutional systems framed according to the Westminster model and with a majority of the populations of African and Asian descent, participating in the same historical push towards self-determination as Asia and Africa, but squeezed geographically between the highly developed and expansive North American continent and the economically underdeveloped Latin American mainland. This sketch of some of the objective determinants of foreign policy reveals four options for the new Caribbean States other than the traditional links with the metropolis.

Firstly, the common bonds established during the eighteenth and nineteenth centuries through forced migration and the joint effort to attain independence call for a political rapprochement with the Afro-Asian group of countries. This is substantiated by the voting behaviour of Jamaica and Trinidad and Tobago in the United Nations General Assembly, particularly on such issues as colonialism and racialism. It is also reflected in the visits of the Prime Minister of Trinidad and Tobago, Dr. Eric Williams, to India in 1961 and to Africa in 1964, in the establishment of a Trinidad Embassy in Addis Ababa, and in the visits to the West Indies of President Leopold Senghor of Senegal, Emperor Haile Selassie of Ethiopia, President Kenneth Kaunda of Zambia, and Prime Minister Indira Gandhi of India.

Secondly, increased relations with the North American continent partly substitute for the declining involvement of the United Kingdom in the Caribbean. The United States and Canada provide new markets for West Indian products, while their private investments and public aid are on the increase. Potential conflicts, such as the liquidation of American military establishments, have been avoided by peaceful settlement and two West Indian countries, Trinidad and Barbados, have joined the hemispheric collective security system.

The third element in the diversification of the foreign relations of West Indian States and Guyana is reflected in the serious attempts made since 1967 to bring about increased intra-regional cooperation and integration. The establishment of the Caribbean Free Trade Association

(CARIFTA) and of the Regional Secretariat on the one hand, and the proposals for the creation of a Caribbean Development Bank and new regional Common Services on the other hand, contain a certain degree of hope that the region can achieve progress in unity despite the failure of the colonial administration to introduce effective and lasting federal structures of government.

Finally, the latest development is to be seen in the increased interest which the West Indies and Guyana begin to attribute to Latin America. In many ways, some Latin American countries respond favourably to Caribbean overtures and a consciousness of common problems and common goals evolves on both sides. Concrete evidence for this is now sufficiently abundant to justify some detached reflection on the subject. The foremost task of the analyst consists in detecting the motives justifying a rapprochement. These might be rather impressive and could actually lead to rash assertions and false hopes. Thus, an inventory of the obstacles to be overcome may help in measuring the scope of the action required by governments, the business community, the universities and voluntary organizations, as well as the period of time which will evolve, before any tangible changes can be discerned.

Evidence of Commonwealth Caribbean Interest in Latin America

The first significant move towards Latin America originated from Trinidad and Tobago after the advent of the People's National Movement (PNM) in 1956. The aim of the PNM was to liquidate a number of disputes which had affected the relations between Great Britain and Venezuela and to initiate a series of cooperative ventures with the latter country. The disputes concerned such matters as the delimitation of territorial waters, illegal immigration, contraband, fishing, and discriminatory trade practices.[2] When Trinidad and Tobago attained independence under the PNM's leadership in 1962, most differences with Venezuela had either been eliminated or their resolution had been agreed upon in principle. Some are still unsolved but have lost their inflammatory attributes. The abolition in 1965 of the thirty per cent surtax previously imposed by Venezuela on the products originating from independent Commonwealth Caribbean countries constituted the major reciprocation of the goodwill policy of the Trinidad Government. It cemented the relations existing between the two countries to an extent which made possible, in June 1967,

---

[2] See Eric Williams, *History of the People of Trinidad and Tobago* (Port-of-Spain: PNM Publishing Company, 1962), pp. 257–259. See also a summary of the efforts undertaken by the Trinidad Government in a speech by the then Premier, Dr. Eric Williams, to the Legislative Council, 28 August, 1959.

the formal constitution of a Mixed Commission whose terms of reference include the preparation of Trinidad's participation in Latin American integrative schemes, expansion of trade, technical cooperation, education, tourism, migration, joint planning in industrialization, and the harmonization of policies with regard to mineral and petroleum resources.[3]

The second major indication of West Indian interest in Latin America again originated from Trinidad and Tobago, when, in 1967, the Government for the first time propagated the idea of a possible entry into a wider Latin American economic institution. The occasion was the Punta del Este Conference of American Presidents where the Prime Minister of Trinidad and Tobago represented his country as the first West Indian member of the Organization of American States. Together with the other Latin American countries, a firm pledge to join in setting up a Latin American Common Market by 1970 was made by the Trinidad Government. This means, as an immediate step, that Trinidad must seek association with a particular Latin American integration bloc which would subsequently be merged with others into the Common Market. The choice is, of course, very limited: apart from the rather remote Central American Common Market, the projected Andean Common Market is the only imaginative and promising integrative scheme in Latin America at the present time.[4] Trinidad has indicated her strong interest in this project, although very little publicity has been given to a possible Andean dimension of her foreign policy.[5] In the meantime, the Andean project itself is not progressing sufficiently due, among other factors, to the articulate opposition professed by the Venezuelan business community.

Participation in the Andean group is, according to the draft Pact, restricted to members of the Latin American Free Trade Association. Consequently, it appears that Trinidad and Tobago will, after all, have to join

---

3 A.N.R. Robinson, *The Foreign Policy of Trinidad and Tobago,* paper presented at the Institute of International Relations, University of the West Indies, St. Augustine, 29 May 1968. The Mixed Commission met in Port-of-Spain in November, 1967, and in Caracas in September, 1968.

4 For an introduction to Andean integration, see Rodrigo Botero, *La Comunidad Económica Caribe-Andina* (Bogotá: Ediciones Tercer Mundo, 1967).

5 In February, 1968, when answering a question from an independent member, the Leader of the Senate only indicated briefly that diplomatic approaches had been made to members of LAFTA and that an invitation to join the Central American Common Market had been received. See *Debates of the Senate* (Hansard) vol. 7, No. 10 (6 February 1968), pp. 612-614. Soon after, the Washington correspondent of a major Caracas newspaper reported that Trinidad was actively preparing to join the Andean Common Market. See "Trinidad Ingresaría en el Grupo Andino de Acelerada Integración", *El Universal,* 17 Febrero 1968, p. 6. An announcement to this effect by an official of the Trinidad Government was made in Caracas on the occasion of the visit of a trade mission in September 1968. See "Trinidad Bids to Join Andean Pact", *Trinidad Guardian,* 13 September, 1968, p. 2.

this wider Latin American group, despite the serious deficiencies in the operation of the scheme admitted by the Latin Americans themselves. Based on a concept of simple trade liberalization which has failed to bring about an expansion of trade and the protection of the interests of less developed members,[6] LAFTA is presently undergoing an "agonizing reappraisal" by the protagonists of Latin American integration. The most recent trade figures reveal that, after a period of stagnation, LAFTA has now entered a phase of regression. Indeed, in 1967, intra-regional trade in Latin America has declined for the first time since the Association was founded.[7] Thus, the joining of LAFTA could in no case constitute an achievement in itself; it becomes merely a formal step designed to open access to the Andean group with the ultimate aim of becoming a part of the proposed Latin American Common Market.

The third significant indication of West Indian interest in Latin America comes from Barbados where, a few months after independence in 1966, a senior minister was appointed to the post of Minister for Caribbean and Latin American Affairs. Having joined the Organization of American States too late to participate in the Punta del Este meeting, the country subsequently professed its intention to seek a transformation of its foreign policy which may be considered to be as far-reaching as the one sought by Trinidad and Tobago.[8] The Prime Minister, Mr. Errol Barrow, in a declaration made at the headquarters of the Organization of American States in September, 1968, went even to the point of asserting that

> Our community of interests now resides with the members of the O. A. S.

Speaking of future links with Great Britain, he said:

> I do not think that anyone in the Western Hemisphere will shed a tear if these connections in the way of trade are severed, because it appears that they will be severed in a unilateral fashion and it is better that we are forewarned and forearmed so that we can make our new alliance with those people who have a community of interests with us.[9]

---

[6] See Sidney Dell, *A Latin American Common Market?* (London: Oxford University Press, 1966), particularly at pp. 70–94; 206–217.

[7] Global trade decreased by 45.2 million dollars (U.S.) or 3.1% in 1967. See "A Monthly Report on Latin American Integration," *Comercio Exterior* (Mexico), XIV, No. 11 (November, 1968), 7.

[8] "LBJ looks forward to Barbados Visit," *Trinidad Guardian,* 13 September 1968, p. 1. Within hours of the adoption of the Punta del Este Resolution, the Prime Minister had announced that Barbados would subscribe to the idea of a Latin American Common Market. See *Sunday Advocate,* 16 April 1967.

[9] If this severance of trade relations actually occurred, Barbados would be plunged into a serious economic crisis. The other Commonwealth Caribbean coun-

Jamaica, whose major post-independence shift in foreign policy was in the direction of the United States and Canada, stretched out a first feeler towards Latin America with the establishment of an embassy in Mexico in 1966. The Prime Minister's report on foreign affairs of that year for the first time mentioned closer links with Latin America as a priority. Plans were made to set up another embassy in Costa Rica, which would also serve Panama, two countries that have traditionally received a strong flow of Jamaican immigrants.[10] In 1968, the Jamaican High Commissioner in Port-of-Spain was also accredited to Venezuela. These moves are only of a preliminary nature and will be followed, if a dynamic Latin American policy is the true aim of the Jamaican Government, by efforts of official and private bodies at increasing trade, cultural relations and, functional cooperation.

In her post-independence attempts to follow the continental vocation which geographical considerations dictate to her, Guyana, the only English-speaking territory on the South American continent, has been severely hampered by Venezuela's claim on a large portion of her territory.[11] However, in September, 1968, she succeeded in establishing closer relations with her other powerful neighbour, Brazil. Apart from the exchange of diplomatic envoys, the two countries agreed on increased commercial and cultural relations and on an improvement of communications.[12] This, incidentally, occurred at about the same time as Trinidad opened a permanent diplomatic mission in Rio de Janeiro. Brazil thus suddenly emerged as a new partner in economic and cultural cooperation for the Eastern Caribbean countries.

While all the above-mentioned efforts are based primarily on economic considerations or on particular political objectives, the independent Commonwealth countries of the Caribbean have also given evidence of a rapprochement with Latin America in their voting behaviour on wider political issues at the United Nations. This observation applies primarily to Trinidad and Jamaica. Both countries identified themselves quite strongly with the Afro-Asian group after their independence in 1962, but

tries have always presented their desire to establish new hemispheric links as an additional, not alternative, dimension of foreign policy. See, Government of Barbados, *Address by the Rt. Hon. Errol W. Barrow at the Protocolary Session of the OAS Council Held in His Honour,* 1968, p. 4.

[10] See Hugh Shearer's report to the House of Representatives, *Activities of the Ministry of External Affairs during the year 1966 and Forecast for 1967/68* (Ministry Paper No. 45, 28 July, 1967).

[11] See below, pp. 258–259.

[12] See *Guyana Journal* (Georgetown: Ministry of External Affairs, 1968) No. 2, pp. 73–76.

later began to operate as effective members of the Latin American group.[13] This was largely the result of the evolution which occurred after the adoption of the Act of Washington in December, 1964, in the attitude of the Latin Americans towards the Commonwealth Caribbean.[14] The change in attitude is striking, when one considers, for instance, that Mr. Robert Lightbourne, Jamaica's representative at UNCTAD in Geneva (1964), together with the representative of Trinidad and Tobago, were rebuffed by the Latin American group when the question of representation on the Trade and Development Board arose, whereas in 1967, Dr. Patrick Solomon, Trinidad's Permanent Delegate to the United Nations, was the President of the Latin American group in the United Nations and introduced, on its behalf, the compromise resolution on the Middle East Crisis. Today, it is a generally accepted practice to include the Commonwealth Caribbean States in the quota granted to Latin America for representation on international bodies. However, on certain specific issues such as colonialism and racialism, particularly in the southern part of Africa, the Commonwealth Caribbean States feel strongly that their first allegiance continues to lie with the Afro-Asian group.

REASONS FOR COMMONWEALTH CARIBBEAN INTEREST IN
LATIN AMERICA

1. Economic Motives

First and foremost among the reasons explaining the new orientation of some Commonwealth Caribbean States is the desire to devise a foreign policy that will promote the general economic well-being of the population by opening markets capable of absorbing indigenous products, by finding supplies at the most advantageous terms, and by obtaining financial and technical support for economic development. It was the threat of Britain's entry into the European Economic Community under terms unfavorable to the Commonwealth which sparked off the search for new economic partners in 1962 and, again, in 1966. Britain, of course, remains the major market for West Indian agricultural products and is a source of aid, but in view of the uncertainty of the E.E.C.'s position on the Commonwealth preferential system, the West Indies had to begin, not only to seek a diversification of trade links, but to plan the restructuralization of their econo-

---

[13] In 1963, when outlining the possible alignments of Trinidad and Tobago with particular blocs within the United Nations, the Prime Minister merely mentioned the Latin American group and elaborated in great detail on the importance of the African group. Cf. *The Foreign Relations of Trinidad and Tobago*, Speech to the House of Representatives, 6 December, 1963 (Port-of-Spain: Government Printing Office, 1963), pp. 5–10.

[14] On the Act of Washington, see below pp. 258–259.

mies in order to make their production compatible with the needs of potential customers and suppliers. The pledge made by the Prime Minister of Trinidad and Tobago at Punta del Este came only months after Britain's second move towards the E.E.C.

An alternative course of action was to follow Britain's initiative and to seek association with the E.E.C. Apart from Jamaica, no Commonwealth Caribbean State considered this possibility in 1966. A realistic assessment of the chances of association leads to the conclusion that the E.E.C. has no interest in accepting the Caribbean States and that the continental European markets are already crowded with most of the products of which the Commonwealth Caribbean is a potential supplier.[15] The only reasonable objective of association would, in fact, be to preserve the privileged position which the Commonwealth Caribbean enjoys on the British market, in the event of British membership in the E.E.C.[16] This, however, is no realistic long-term objective, as preferential systems linking an individual E.E.C. member to an outside group are bound to be either rejected at the time of admission or phased out rapidly. The bargaining position of Britain in the E.E.C. is rather weak and, despite present assertions to the contrary, will not be exhausted by Britain for a cause which ranks merely among her secondary objectives on the agenda of negotiation with the E.E.C. It would be advisable to remember that twice within five years, Britain was ready to relinquish her position in the European Free Trade Association for membership in the E.E.C. after repeatedly asserting her solidarity with the "Outer Seven."

The foregoing is not intended to mean that efforts at increasing exports to Britain and to the European continent or at obtaining European aid should not be pursued by the governments, business companies or Chambers of Commerce in the Commonwealth Caribbean. On the contrary, there are concrete possibilities of increased economic relations which could be explored much in the same way as in the case of the United States and Canada. The difference with the attempts at closer relations with Latin America is, however, that the economic partners in the developed world, although they may for a long time to come be the most important customers and suppliers, are not prepared to enter into any new, strong, institutional arrangements. The trend in present-day economic policies is towards the liquidation of preferential systems which are an outcome of

---

15 On this point, see the study by the West India Committee, *The Commonwealth Caribbean and the European Economic Community* (London, 1967).

16 Jamaica's position is explained by a stronger dependence on the British market than that of the other Caribbean States. See the statement of the Jamaican Prime Minister, Mr. Hugh Shearer, to the House of Representatives after a visit to Britain, France, Holland and Germany, 2 November, 1967.

colonial or other special relationships,[17] and the establishment of re
groupings among developing countries to balance some of the losse
fered from the gradual closure of traditional markets.

The negative effect of Britain's disengagement from the Caribb
not the sole motive for a reorientation of West Indian and Guyanese foreign policy. Latin America has enough potential to become an attractive
economic partner in its own right. Its population will expand to approximately 600 million by the end of the century and its purchasing power is
expected to grow at the rate of 5% per annum.[18]

With regard to economic aid, it must be noted that the participation
of Commonwealth Caribbean States in regional integrative schemes promises to lead to additional assistance from the United States. It is a well-
known fact that President Johnson encouraged the willingness of Latin
American leaders to cooperate among themselves with promises of additional development funds from the United States.[19] Similarly, Caribbean
integration has received the support of Britain, the United States, and
Canada in the form of contributions to the regional Development Bank.
Furthermore, should the United States eventually agree to establish a preferential hemispheric trade system as a new form of aid, despite present
trends against the concept, it would be of the utmost importance for the
Commonwealth Caribbean to be part of such an arrangement.

As for private foreign investments, membership in a Latin American
Common Market may permit Caribbean countries to end the under-
utilization of their production lines for manufactures, which results from
the smallness of their markets.[20] Foreign investors are already attracted to
the English-speaking countries by virtue of easier communication, exceptionally high literacy rates and political stability. The prospect of being
able to cater from such a base for Latin American markets may constitute
an important additional incentive to invest.[21]

---

[17] For an analysis of the reasons for which even the beneficiaries of preferences
should work towards the liquidation of such a system, see Alister McIntyre, "Decolonization and Trade Policy," *The Caribbean in Transition* (Puerto Rico: Institute
of Caribbean Studies, 1965), pp. 196–200.

[18] See the reports of the Economic Commission for Latin America, for instance, the annual *Economic Survey of Latin America*, published by the United Nations, New York.

[19] Meeting of American Chiefs of State, *Declaration of the Presidents of
America*, Punta del Este, April, 1967 (Washington: Organization of American
States, 1967).

[20] This may be difficult in the short run since most Latin American countries
have completed their import substitution programme. See Alister McIntyre, *op. cit.*
pp. 208-209. McIntyre argues that the low degree of import substitution in the Commonwealth Caribbean makes regional integration among Caribbean countries more
attractive than an association with Latin America.

[21] See Frank Dowdy, "OAS vs ECM: Can We Manage Both?" *Enterprise*

On still a very small scale, Trinidad's efforts at improving its trade balance with Venezuela are beginning to produce results. The meetings of the Mixed Commission, other negotiations for trade concessions and several exploratory missions of business representatives are bound, in not too distant a future, to increase these gains to a tangible size. Other countries may discover that bilateral arrangements of the same kind are effective in bringing about short-term gains. Thus, there is scope for making a partnership with Latin America a proposition of immediate interest, despite the fact that structural problems will probably account for the postponement of substantial benefits to the long-run perspective.

Since any association between sovereign states must be solidly grounded on mutual interests, it is necessary to briefly point out that Latin America may also expect substantial benefits from increased relations with the Commonwealth Caribbean. Foremost among the elements which West Indian negotiators may throw into the balance are the relatively high purchasing power of the Commonwealth Caribbean equivalent to that of the much larger Central American region, and the low degree to which the import substitution process has been completed in the Caribbean. Furthermore, Latin America, as evidenced by the Table on page 263 has a very large export surplus towards the Caribbean. The beneficiary countries, Venezuela and Columbia, may find it desirable to consolidate their privileged position as oil suppliers by influencing the behaviour of international oil companies through inter-governmental arrangements with the oil-importing countries. Finally, the Caribbean is an important source of bauxite and laterites and constitutes the natural partner in the development of Latin America's metallurgic industry.

2. Political Motives

In the balkanized third world, the search for a united front defending the interests of the new states and, in some cases, of the other developing countries, is an essential objective of foreign policy. It explains the solidarity, which all West Indian leaders have proclaimed at one stage or another, with the Afro-Asian countries. It also explains, to some extent, the efforts for regional integration in the Caribbean and the new orientation towards Latin America. However, politically, and even more so, economically, the trends towards Afro-Asian solidarity appear to offer little concrete advantage to the newly independent West Indian States and Guyana. Trade relations are seriously hampered by the cost of transportation. On the political scene, the African and Asian states have only limited opportunities

(Trinidad and Tobago Federation of Chambers of Industry and Commerce Inc., December, 1967), p. 19.

to reciprocate the support received in the United Nations from Caribbean states. On the other hand, the Caribbean itself has no weight as a separate part of the third world under the pressure of Western or Eastern power politics. This is true, not only because of the fragmentation of the Caribbean into English-, French-, Spanish-, and Dutch-speaking parts, but also in view of the more real than apparent rift between Jamaica and the rest of the Commonwealth Caribbean.

The desire to manifest strength through unity naturally points towards an increased alignment with Latin America for the joint defense of common interests on the international scene. The most important such interest is in the field of security. It entails for each Latin American state protection from extra-hemispheric aggression, from unilateral intervention by the United States and from aggression by another Latin American state. The present solution for collective security is the system adopted by the Organization of American States. The Rio Treaty of 1947 protects signatories from extra-regional or mutual aggression. It does not, however, eliminate the danger of unilateral U.S. action, and it is particularly in this respect that the unity of the other states in the hemisphere may be of vital importance.

One of the more recent threats to the security of the established regimes in the hemisphere comes through subversive activities encouraged by the Castro Government in Cuba. Venezuela is a declared target of guerrilla warfare supported by Cuba and therefore has an active interest in obtaining the cooperation of Trinidad, which has traditionally served as a springboard for infiltrators.[22] But West Indian leaders themselves are fearful of Communist subversion and make no secret of their desire to resist such activities, if necessary in cooperation with other states in the hemisphere.

It is interesting to note that the rapprochement of the Commonwealth Caribbean with Latin America has been paralleled by increased relations with the United States. Membership in the Organization of American States has been widely interpreted in the West Indies as a move towards Latin America, although its major objective was the participation in hemispheric collective security and aid programmes, which are founded primarily upon the military potential and the financial resources of the United

---

[22] This is true even in the most recent past according to a report in the Venezuelan press. See "Agentes subversives entraron por Trinidad," *El Universal* (Caracas), 10 November, 1968. On 24 September, 1967, the Minister of External Affairs of Trinidad and Tobago told the 12th Meeting of Consultation of Foreign Ministers of the OAS, that Trinidad stood firmly with Venezuela in the conflict with Cuba.

States. In fact, the increasing influence of the United States in the Commonwealth Caribbean cannot be separated from the rapprochement between the latter and Latin America. The entry into the Organization of American States serves a variety of purposes, some of which can be attained in partnership with the United States, some in cooperation with Latin America and some by the Organization as a whole.[23] The power vacuum and the economic difficulties which are a result of Britain's disengagement from the Caribbean cannot be compensated for by the Latin American countries, which lack the military capability and the economic resources to provide an immediate alternative. Interestingly enough, strategic and financial considerations are forcing the United States to liquidate her military bases in the West Indies at the very moment of the disengagement from the same area by a friendly extra-hemispheric power. The removal of American troops from the Chaguaramas base, a major element in the control of the Southern Caribbean, may be partly responsible for Trinidad's entry into the OAS, which now extends collective security to an area previously controlled by the United States and Britain. One may speculate about whether this actually means that the United States will, in the future, pursue its interests in the Caribbean with a multilateral blessing. One might think that the United States would hesitate to expose itself again to the hostility of Latin America, which resulted from the originally unilateral intervention in the Dominican Republic in 1965. On the other hand, the action of the Soviet Union in Czechoslovakia, endorsed from the outset by a regional collective security system, gives new strength to the concept of the "immediate spheres of interest," in which either the Soviet Union or the United States are unrestricted in the choice of means for the attainment of vital goals.

The establishment of closer links with the United States is not necessarily a popular idea in the Commonwealth Caribbean. The feeling of substituting one form of foreign domination for another and the unpleasant experiences suffered by many black West Indians in the United States account for the limited enthusiasm which large segments of the West Indian public are able to generate for this development. However, Commonwealth Caribbean Governments have little choice in the matter. They welcome the opportunity which the new relations with Latin America offer to them to balance the increased presence of the United States exercised directly or through the Organization of American States.

---

[23] The motives of OAS membership are in themselves worthy of a separate study and will not be further explored here.

OBSTACLES TO A RAPPROACHEMENT OF THE COMMONWEALTH CARIBBEAN AND LATIN AMERICA

1. Political Obstacles

The history of the last 150 years had divided the West Indies and Latin America into two entirely separate worlds. Up to 1797 Trinidad was an integral part of the same Spanish Empire as Venezuela. Today, it is a country with a different language, a different population and a different political system.

The struggle between monarchism and republicanism, which was won by the latter ideology through the conversion of the Western Hemisphere in the late eighteenth and early nineteenth centuries, has left a barrier between the West Indies and Latin America until the very recent past. Most Latin Americans were somewhat reluctant to accept the membership in the Organization of American States of Commonwealth countries with a governmental system based on the concept of constitutional monarchy. They had a vague feeling that no state could claim to be truly independent as long as the Queen of England remained its Head. When the Charter of the Organization of American States was drawn up in 1948, the possibility of membership for countries other than the United States and the Latin American Republics was not present in the minds of the draftsmen. Article 3 of the Charter merely referred to the possibility of a "new political entity that arises from the union of several Members" becoming a new member in the place of its composite parts. Awareness of Canada's special position emerged much later and the need to adopt a proper procedure for the admission of new members was only fully realized after the independence of Jamaica and Trinidad. The idea that Latin American countries were generally favourable to the Commonwealth Caribbean during the negotiations leading to the adoption of the Act of Washington in 1964 can hardly be accepted.[24] In fact, the opposition was so substantial that an Associated Press report from Washington in October, 1964, quoted "diplomatic sources" as saying that Trinidad would probably complain to the United Nations if the Organization of American

---

[24] Charles Fenwick argues that "From the discussions attending the possible membership of Canada in the Organization, it would appear that membership in the British Commonwealth of Nations would not be an obstacle. On the occasion of Jamaica's independence, August 6, 1962, the Secretary-General of the OAS sent his congratulations and expressed the hope that emergence as a new State may be a first step which could ultimately lead to its incorporation in the American community of nations." See *The Organization of American States* (Washington, 1963), p. 83. The cable of congratulations was actually a compromise after a heated debate in the Council had persuaded the Secretary-General not to accept the invitation of the British Government to attend the independence celebrations personally.

States was unable to fulfill its role as a regional organization by failing to provide rules for the admission of new members.[25]

Monarchism, membership in the Commonwealth, the Queen, and other historical and temperamental differences between the countries and peoples are only partial motives for Latin American suspicions about the new Caribbean states. The major sources of antagonism are disputes over former or present British territories in the hemisphere. Guatemala's claim over the entire territory of British Honduras (Belize), Venezuela's claim over two-thirds of the territory of Guyana and Argentina's claim over the Falkland Islands have resulted in a provision included in the Act of Washington (§ 3) according to which no political entity can be admitted to the Organization of American States "whose territory, in whole or in part, is subject, prior to the date of this resolution, to litigation or claim between an extra-continental country and one or more member States of the Organization of American States, until the dispute has been ended by some peaceful procedure." [26] Guatemala, in particular, has persisted in reserving its position on Belize. In 1955, it ratified the Inter-American Treaty of Reciprocal Assistance with the following reservation:

> The present Treaty poses no impediment whatever to Guatemala's assertion of its rights over the Guantemalan territory of Belize by whatever means it considers most appropriate; . . .[27]

It is quite obvious from the behaviour of a number of Latin American states that the admission of the new Caribbean States constituted a potential threat to the validity of their arguments about the illegality of some British territorial conquests in the hemisphere. It is partly because of Jamaica's and Trinidad's independence that Venezuela, Argentina, and Guatemala have raised their territorial claims in the United Nations since 1962.

While the Act of Washington has opened the way for the admission of Trinidad and Barbados and the establishment of good relations between

---

[25] *Trinidad Guardian*, 7 October, 1964. The Act of Washington was adopted in December, 1964. Already on 6 December, 1963, the Prime Minister of Trinidad and Tobago had said that ". . . there has been . . . a certain resentment that our rights were being tampered with, that our rights as a member of the American family are not recognized, and that we have to depend upon what ultimately appears to be something as of grace, instead of, as we insist, on something as of right." *The Foreign Relations of Trinidad and Tobago*, Speech to the House of Representatives (Port-of-Spain: Government Printing Office, 1963), p. 15.

[26] See Gordon Connell-Smith, *The Inter-American System* (London: Oxford University Press, 1966), p. 298. The three major claims were restated in an appendix to the Final Act.

[27] See *ibid*, p. 192.

these countries and Latin America, it has also created much uncertainty with regard to the security of Belize and Guyana. It is not appropriate at this point to speculate on the future of Belize, which is in a most delicate position after the rejection, by all sides, of the U.S. mediation attempt. The case of Guyana, already an independent country, is as good an illustration for the difficulties which must still be overcome. The security of Guyana is not guaranteed effectively at the present moment. The 1966 Geneva Agreement with Britain and Venezuela, which calls for a peaceful settlement of the dispute, has already been broken by Venezuela with the occupation of the Ankoko Island in 1967 and the extension of Venezuela's territorial waters in 1968.[28] The other Commonwealth Caribbean countries are themselves interested in developing good relations with Venezuela. Britain and the United States have given no unilateral assurances to protect the territorial integrity of Guyana. The support which Guyana may obtain from an Afro-Asian majority in the United Nations is of little practical significance in the face of possible military aggression committed by Venezuela.

The question may be raised whether Guyana could become a party to the Inter-American Treaty of Reciprocal Assistance without being a member of the OAS and receive OAS support in case of a crisis. Although there is no legal provision in the Rio Treaty debarring a non-member of the OAS from undertaking the obligations set forth in the Treaty, it is most unlikely that a majority of OAS members would support Guyana's stand. An indication of this can be seen in the fact that Guyana and Belize are excluded from the efforts to guarantee the de-nuclearization of Latin America. The Treaty for the Prohibition of Nuclear Weapons in Latin America, which was negotiated under the auspices of the United Nations, contains, in identical terms, the provision embodied in paragraph 3 of the Act of Washington for the exclusion of countries whose territory is under dispute.[29]

Thus, despite the position of the United States and several Latin American countries, the claims of Venezuela, Guatemala, and Argentina are a living reality and will increasingly affect the relations between the newly independent Caribbean States and Latin America. A recent incident in the United Nations shows how Caribbean countries whose territory is undisputed can also be drawn into the quarrels of the others.

---

[28] The Venezuelan Decree of 9 July, 1968, annexes a belt of sea lying along the coast of Guyana between the Essequibo River and Waini Point. See *Guyana/Venezuela Relations* (Georgetown: Ministry of External Affairs, 1968), p. 20.

[29] Article 25, section 2. See *Guyana Journal* (Georgetown: Ministry of External Affairs, 1968), No. 1, pp. 29–31, on the protest made by the Guyana Government in the General Assembly of the United Nations.

Barbados was a candidate for membership of the Committee of 24 [30] in which her presence would have been particularly useful, since it discusses annually the situation in the Eastern Caribbean. However, the President of the General Assembly, who happened to be the Foreign Minister of Guatemala, somewhat arbitrarily appointed Ecuador to serve on the Committee. He may have felt that an English-speaking Caribbean country would lend its support to the point of view of Belize in forthcoming debates. The Government of Barbados did not hide its disapproval and protested strongly, together with the other Commonwealth Caribbean States. Guyana felt particularly perturbed, since its Permanent Representative to the United Nations, although at the time the President of the Latin American group, was not consulted on the matter.[31]

It must be clearly underlined that membership in any of the Latin American regional groups does not presuppose membership in the Organization of American States. Article 59 of the Montevideo Treaty, for instance, provides simply for the admission to LAFTA of "Latin American States," a term which in now generally interpreted to include Commonwealth Caribbean States. Quite apart from the legal provisions, it is, however, possible to imagine that members of LAFTA and the CACM might oppose the admission to the LACM of Guyana and Belize on the same political grounds as they oppose admission to the OAS However, there is at present no indication that they will do so or that their point of view would find the support of other Latin American states.

A new element in present-day international relations which may also affect the relations between the Commonwealth Caribbean and

[30] Special Committee on the Situation with regard to the Implementation of the Declaration on the Granting of Independence to Colonial Countries and Peoples, established by General Assembly resolutions 1514 (XV), 1654 (XVI), 1810 (XVII), and 1956 (XVIII).

[31] According to the *Trinidad Guardian* of 29 October, 1968 ("W.I. States Take Offence in UN"), the Deputy Prime Minister of Barbados, Mr. Cameron Tudor, said: ". . . it would be most unfortunate if countries like mine, eager to cooperate with our neighbours on the mainland and in the Spanish-speaking Caribbean, were to gain the impression that there are signs of systematic discrimination against those countries which do not belong to the Iberian tradition." The Barbados *Advocate-News* of 28 October ("Barbados in UN Issue"), not representing an official view, went much further: "Informed Caribbean sources, pointing out that this was not the first occasion that the 22-nation group had been divided between its old white Spanish-speaking countries and the newly independent English-speaking black countries, said it was quite possible that four Caribbean countries might soon leave the regional group and join the Afro-Asian group." To support its argument that there is discrimination within the Latin American group along linguistic and racial lines, the commentator points out that Haiti and Brazil were not consulted when the appointment was made. In the case of Brazil, this may be due to the fact that ". . . it was sympathetic towards Guyana in its dispute with Venezuela."

Latin America is the mini-state issue. With the admission of Barbados to the OAS, the Latin American countries have acknowledged the concept of the mini-state within the Organization.[32] A few of the Organization's members actually began to realize the implications of this step only after the debate on admission had started. At that stage, they preferred not to make their real feelings known for reasons of international courtesy. The fact remains, however, that a number of Latin American countries are now concerned about the proliferation of statehood in the eastern Caribbean if the present trend results in the application for membership of approximately a dozen islands with a population of less than a hundred thousand inhabitants each. This would bring about a dramatic change in the balance of the English and Spanish/Portugese-speaking members. A situation of this kind is bound to stir up usually dormant suspicions in the minds of the Latin Americans. Their major fear, which may not be altogether unjustified, is that a small Caribbean island emerging from British colonial rule may align itself too easily to the U.S. point of view in controversial issues arising between North and South America.

If the admission of new mini-states to the Organization of American States is brought up again, the Latin Americans may have themselves partly to blame. The reason for this is that, much as the United Nations in the Committee of 24, the OAS has actively promoted the idea of complete and separate independence of all territories regardless of size and population. While the United Nations is motivated by the principle of self-determination and by the strong anti-colonialist feelings of a majority of members, the OAS acted primarily on the basis of the principle of noninterference in hemispheric affairs enshrined in the Monroe Doctrine. Neither the UN nor the OAS has ever given priority to the creation of regional groupings of dependent territories over the attainment of independence as separate island-states. As far back as 1948, the Ninth International Conference of American States in Bogotá called for the creation of an American Committee on Dependent Territories, which carried out substantial research on the various territories involved.[33] In the Final Act, signed at Havana in 1949, the Committee resolved:

> To address to the non-American countries having possessions in America a request for their cooperation with a view to definitive solution of the colonial problem on the basis of the

[32] See Patricia Wohlegemuth-Blair, *The Ministate Dilemma* (New York: Carnegie Endowment for International Peace, 1967), who suggests a population of less than 300,000 people as a criterion to define the mini-state.

[33] See Comisión Americana de Territorios Dependientes, *Memoria/Informe*, 2 vols., (La Habana, 1949).

principles of democracy and liberty, to the end that their colonies and possessions may be established as independent and democratic states.[34]

The recommendations and resolutions of the Committee were subsequently endorsed and expanded at the Fourth Meeting of Consultation of Ministers of Foreign Affairs of the OAS (Washington, 1951) and at the Tenth Inter-American Conference of the OAS (Caracas, 1954). There is no doubt that the OAS must be commended for thus lending strong support to the process of decolonization as a whole and in the hemisphere in particular. However, the point must be stressed that the Organization, by failing to call initially for the creation of larger units, has encouraged a movement towards the proliferation of mini-states which may ultimately have an adverse effect on its own operations and lead to serious quarrels among members on the question of admission and voting rights.

2. Economic Obstacles

Three major economic obstacles are in the way of the integration of the Commonwealth Caribbean with Latin America: the traditional links of the West Indies and Guyana with the Commonwealth, the incompatibility of the economies from a static point of view, and the lack of cohesion of CARIFTA with regard to the foreign economic policies of members.[35]

From the point of view of the Latin Americans, the Commonwealth preferential system is a serious obstacle to regional integration. Manufactured goods purchased in Latin America are already quite uncompetitive in view of the high tariff protection which most producers have traditionally enjoyed. To come up with a product which is not only internationally competitive but which can outdo, in quality and price, the Commonwealth goods admitted to the West Indies and Guyana at preferential customs tariff is a matter of impossibility for practically every Latin American manufacturer.

The West Indian business community maintains close links with

---

[34] *Final Act of the American Committee on Dependent Territories,* signed at Habana on 21 July, 1949 (Washington: Pan American Union, 1949), Congress and Conference Series No. 60, p. 10.

[35] One might add to this the present protectionist policies adopted by Latin American countries as well as a host of other factors which are impediments to the integration of Latin America itself. These elements cannot be adequately dealt with here. See Sidney Dell, *A Latin American Common Market?* (London: Oxford University Press, 1966); Miguel Wionczek (Ed.), *Latin American Economic Integration* (New York: Praeger, 1966).

British and North American suppliers and customers. The expansion of trade with Latin America requires better travel facilities and telecommunications. Bankers must gain faith in new partners. Clerks must learn to calculate in meters and kilos. Everyone encounters the language barrier. It may take ten to twenty years to make the adjustments necessary to overcome these difficulties.

TRADE WITH LATIN AMERICA[36]

	Imports			Exports		
TRINIDAD ($ mill. TT.)	1956	1961	1965	1956	1961	1965
Trade with Latin America	81.6	144.1	204.4	19.4	19.1	20.2
Total Trade	301.5	584.5	817.0	330.2	593.9	690.5
Percentage of Latin America in Total Trade	27.1%	24.7%	25.0%	5.9%	3.2%	2.9%
JAMAICA (£ mill.)						
Trade with Latin America	1.1	1.5	9.5	.12	.06	1.0
Total Trade	58.3	75.4	105.0	39.3	61.5	76.7
Percentage of Latin America in Total Trade	1.8%	2.0%	9.1%	.31%	.10%	1.3%
BARBADOS ($ mill. E.C.)						
Trade with Latin America	n.a.	3.1	13.0	n.a.	.02	.01
Total Trade	n.a.	80.3	116.2	n.a.	43.3	64.2
Percentage of Latin America in Total Trade	n.a.	3.9%	11.2%	n.a.	.05%	.02%
GUYANA ($ mill. G.)						
Trade with Latin America	.37	3.1	0.7	.21	1.0	1.6
Total Trade	99.9	146.5	178.8	94.7	148.3	166.7
Percentage of Latin America in Total Trade	.37%	2.1%	.40%	.22%	.69%	.94%

[36] Trinidad: *The Balance of Payments of Trinidad and Tobago 1956–65* (Port-of-Spain: Central Statistical Office, 1968) and *Overseas Trade 1956, 1961, 1965* (Port-of-Spain: Central Statistical Office, 1957, 1962, 1966).

Jamaica: *External Trade of Jamaica 1956, 1961, 1965* (Kingston: Department of Statistics, 1958, 1962, 1966).

Barbados: *Overseas Trade—1961 and 1965* (Bridgetown: Statistical Service, 1962 and 1966).

Guyana: *Annual Account Relating to External Trade, 1956, 1961* (Georgetown: Department of Customs and Excise, 1957, 1962).

For more details on Caribbean-Latin American Trade, see Alister McIntyre "Aspects of Development and Trade in the Commonwealth Caribbean", *Economic Bulletin for Latin America*, X, No. 2 (October, 1965), 149–150; 161–162.

Importers in the Commonwealth Caribbean can take advantage of the export credit facilities offered by the developed countries. No Latin American country has, at present, the financial resources and the promotional attitude to set up equivalent facilities with a view to outdoing the traditional suppliers. The same can be said of the West Indian producers who are interested in getting a foothold in the Latin American market.

The impact of traditional links, acquired habits and metropolitan advantages is clearly reflected in the foreign trade statistics of Commonwealth Caribbean States. For those observers who adopt a static point of view, the discussion on Caribbean-Latin American integration reaches a final deadlock when the figures of interregional trade are revealed. The Table shows that, in 1965, the Commonwealth Caribbean States sent between 0.02 per cent (Barbados) and 2.9 per cent (Trinidad) of their total exports to Latin America, which is indeed quite negligible. The only substantial Latin American trade connection of any Caribbean country is reflected by the heavy imports by Trinidad of crude oil from Venezuela and Colombia. (This element reappears in Trinidad's balance of trade through exports of refined oil to North America). All four countries, incidentally, have an unfavourable balance of trade towards Latin America. Trinidad, Barbados, and Jamaica have substantially increased their imports, while exports have remained insignificant.

The static interpretation of trade statistics is, of course, not satisfactory. The fact that a country has a high export rate to another country does not mean that the two must become part of an institutional arrangement for integration. The traditional markets for the exports of Commonwealth Caribbean States must be safeguarded through the maintenance of quality standards at competitive prices, commodity agreements, and economic policies which permit export-oriented firms to function adequately. On the other hand, a low export rate is not an impediment to integration. The entire concept of trade expansion through regional integration is obviously based on a dynamic view of production and export promotion.[37] The attempt to reduce the reliance on exports of primary products to developed countries by an increase in exports of manufactured goods to developing countries is the only feasible avenue for developing countries in the light of high protection and competition in the markets for manufactured goods of the developed countries. But this solution requires an enormous effort on behalf of the participating countries, such as regional coordination of development plans, improve-

---

[37] United Nations Conference on Trade and Development, *Trade Expansion and Economic Integration among Developing Countries,* TD/B/85, 2 August, 1966.

ment of communications, complementarity agreements, allocation of investments, and, above all, a promotional export policy on behalf of both governments and private circles.

From a static point of view, it is correct to assert that export crops, such as sugar, citrus, and bananas, which because of the labour-intensive production process are of the greatest significance to the economic well-being and political stability of the West Indies, have no future in Latin American markets. In fact, all Latin American countries are either self-sufficient in the production of these crops or cover their needs through imports from neighbouring countries. If the West Indies, rather than enjoying quantitative protection and preferential prices on the British market, had to compete with Latin America on free world markets, they would encounter the most serious economic difficulties. To this extent, the incompatibility of West Indian and Latin American economies is real and cannot be resolved in the short-run. Integration must therefore be directed primarily at the increased exchange of manufactured goods, raw materials, oil, chemicals and processed foodstuff.

Current trade statistics do not reflect indirect interregional trade resulting from the corporate integration of sources of raw materials in one region, processing plants in a developed economy, and markets in the other region. Thus, for example, Latin America covers its imports of aluminium mainly through purchases from American and Canadian companies, which extract bauxite and alumina in the Caribbean and process it in North America.[38] The economic integration of the two regions may create an incentive for foreign companies to establish local processing plants and thus bring about a substantial increase in direct interregional trade.

The problem of integration with Latin America is further complicated by the attempt of some Commonwealth Caribbean countries to obtain simultaneous affiliation with various integrative schemes, which is due to differences in the structure of their foreign economic relations. At present, only Trinidad and Barbados are committed to participation in the future Latin American attempts at integration. Jamaica is still looking towards the E.E.C. and is a very lukewarm supporter of Caribbean integration. Guyana is excluded from the Latin club and sees Commonwealth and Caribbean ties as the only immediate solution. Trinidad and Barbados will face a very serious dilemma when called upon to participate

---

[38] See Norman Girvan and Owen Jefferson, "Institutional Arrangements and the Economic Integration of the Caribbean and Latin America." Paper presented at a Conference on International Relations at Mona (Jamaica), April, 1967, mimeographed, p. 13.

in the establishment of the Latin American Common Market: either they will succeed in both persuading Jamaica to go along and eliminating Latin resistance against Guyana and Belize, thus allowing for CARIFTA to be associated with Latin America as a regional formation, or the future of CARIFTA will become highly precarious. The simultaneous affiliation of Trinidad and Barbados with the Commonwealth, CARIFTA, and the LACM will, in itself, create some, although not insurmountable, difficulties with the Latin Americans. However, if Jamaica, as a member of CARIFTA were to gain associate status with the E.E.C. rather than following the other Commonwealth Caribbean countries, some intricate technical problems would arise. For instance, to the extent that the control of origin would not be effectively enforced, goods produced in the E.E.C. could be imported into Latin America through CARIFTA at preferential tariffs without reciprocity for Latin America on the E.E.C. market. But even if Jamaica's plea for association with the E.E.C. is unsuccessful, as it will probably be, the unity of CARIFTA is threatened by Jamaica's lack of interest in Latin America. If Trinidad and Barbados were to be the only members to join the LACM, the evolution of CARIFTA from a free trade association to an economic union, which is an avowed aim of the group, comes to an end. Indeed, the formulation of a common foreign economic policy of CARIFTA would then be incompatible with the obligation of Trinidad and Barbados to adopt the foreign economic policy of the LACM.

On a similar line of thought, the continued formal dependence of the smaller CARIFTA countries on Britain may complicate the Association's relationship with Latin America. Members of the East Caribbean Common Market (Antigua, Dominica, Grenada, St. Lucia, St. Kitts-Nevis-Anguilla, St. Vincent) which forms a sub-regional group within CARIFTA, and Montserrat have certain special relationships with Britain. Their currency, the East Caribbean dollar, is linked to sterling in such a way that devaluation of the latter extends automatically to the former.[39] In a general way, their right to decide on foreign economic policy is restricted by their status as colonies (Bahamas, Montserrat, St. Vincent) or by the new arrangements for associated statehood with Britain (Antigua, Dominica, Grenada, St. Lucia, St. Kitts-Nevis-Anguilla). This, then, is a major handicap for participation in the elaboration of a

---

[39] For the functioning of the East Caribbean Currency Board, see Clive Thomas, *Monetary and Financial Arrangements in a Dependent Monetary Economy* (Mona: Institute of Social and Economic Research, 1965), pp. 15–36.

common foreign economic policy within a larger Caribbean or Latin American unit.[40]

CONCLUSION

When choosing an order of presentation of the motives for, and obstacles to, increased relations between the Commonwealth Caribbean and Latin America, we have been guided by the conviction that *economic motives* are the prime force behind any new developments and that the *political obstacles* appear to be particularly strong at the present time. This observation is a source of moderate optimism about the feasibility of increased relations. Indeed, as long as economic reasons motivate the need for cooperation, the chances of tangible results are reasonable. This is illustrated by the success of regional economic groupings whose members had just emerged from a mutual war (European Economic Community) or where a break in diplomatic relations among some members had little effect on the functioning of common institutions (Central American Common Market). Where economic needs dictate a certain course of action, political obstacles can be overcome. The opposite situation, where a political drive for unity faces serious economic obstacles, has not usually permitted the attainment of satisfactory results. Evidence for this can be seen in the collapse of federal structures that had not equipped the central government with the resources and instruments needed to ensure the economic well-being and the harmonious development of the entire group (Federation of the West Indies, United Arab Republic).

The information available to policy-makers in the West Indies and Latin America on the potentialities of present and future relations is still scarce. Many problems need to be studied and we shall subsequently indicate a few avenues for research. But the elements that are presently known and have been, to some extent, explored here allow us to indicate a few points which must be foremost in the minds of future analysts as well as some tentative conclusions.

1. The most striking feature in the foreign economic policies of the West Indian States and Guyana is, despite occasional utterances to the contrary, the preservation of preferential treatment for sugar, citrus, and bananas on the British market. A limitation of the imports of these products by Britain and a reduction of preferential prices would create addi-

---

[40] For details on division of power between Britain and the Associated States in the field of foreign affairs, see Margaret Broderick, "Associated Statehood–A New Form of Decolonisation," *The International and Comparative Law Quarterly*, 17, Part 2 (April 1968), 375–383.

tional massive unemployment in the West Indies and, quite certainly, serious political turmoil. Only two alternatives exist for British preferences on agricultural crops. One is to obtain similar preferences on the markets of other developed countries, i.e., in fact, in the United States and Canada. Attempts to this effect have had limited success so far. The other consists of diversifying agricultural production by giving priority to goods which can be consumed locally, e.g., rice and soya beans, and to light manufactured goods for the export market. This requires an enormous human and financial effort and will take more than the few years that are left until the expiration of the Commonwealth Sugar Agreement (1947). [41] Thus, Latin America provides no solution for what West Indian leaders consider their most vital and immediate concern in foreign economic relations.

2. The rapprochement with Latin America, which is almost exclusively explained by certain economic motives, must be clearly separated from the entry of West Indian States into the Organization of American States, which derives primarily from the desire to establish closer relations with the United States, to become part of a collective security system, and to benefit from inter-American aid programmes. Although the decision to establish a Latin American Common Market was taken at an OAS Conference, membership in the two organizations will not be identical (since the United States will not be part of the LACM) and conditions of admission may vary as well.

3. West Indians, who are so well aware of the individual personality of each Caribbean island, are only just discovering that Latin America is not a monolithic bloc. Brazil, with more than one-third of Latin America's population and almost half of South America's territory is, in every respect, very different from the rest of the area. There is a clear cultural affinity between Brazil and the West Indies. It is in these two areas that the world's only harmonious multi-racial societies have been established. Brazil has phenomenal economic potential and will by itself have a population of 200 million people by the turn of the century. It is also the only Latin American country to have a common border with a Commonwealth Caribbean State, Guyana, without challenging the territorial status quo. Being itself interested in opposing territorial claims that may be brought up by Colombia, Venezuela, Guyana, Surinam, or French Guiana, Brazil

---

41 Under the new arrangements made in London in December, 1968, Britain may withdraw from the Agreement in 1974 if she joins the European Economic Community, but not without endeavouring to seek other means to fulfill her present obligations. *The Financial Times,* 4 December, 1968, p. 4.

may, in the interest of hemispheric peace and security, play the role of a counterweight to Venezuela in the territorial dispute over Guyana.[42]

Among the Spanish-speaking countries, there are also enormous differences with which West Indians are to familiarize themselves. Nationalism is a particularly strong force in Latin America and the difficulties which such countries as Venezuela, Colombia, and Peru experience in their mutual relations are in no way minor to the obstacles encountered in the establishment of closer relations with the Commonwealth Caribbean.

4. The establishment of new relations with countries that were totally alien under the regime of colonial bilateralism is a challenging task which cannot be undertaken successfully with the traditional methods of diplomacy. It is simply not enough to exchange envoys who open up costly offices and indulge in cocktail-diplomacy and report-writing. Developing countries need a new type of utilitarian diplomat, with a more aggressive and promotional attitude, capable of handling intricate trade and investment problems. This can be achieved, on the one hand, through adequate training of personnel, and, on the other hand, through appropriate directives emanating from the Ministry of External Affairs in close cooperation with the Ministries of Planning and Development, Finance, Industry, and Commerce. The Venezuela-Trinidad Mixed Commission is the only concrete reflection of such a new formula in the conduct of diplomacy in the context of West Indies-Latin American relations.

5. While the condition of recent independence implies and allows for a general reappraisal of foreign relations, Commonwealth Caribbean States have to achieve a more fundamental reorientation and have more options than most other newly independent States. An evaluation of the performance of the four countries in the face of this challenge can be based on the criteria of dynamism and realism. Trinidad and Tobago rates extremely well in that it has not only explored all feasible alternatives, but has attributed the correct relative significance to the available options. Barbados has also manifested much dynamism, but has sometimes put an unrealistic emphasis on Latin America in its foreign policy pronouncements. Guyana, again, has displayed exceptional dynamism in exploring all possible avenues, but its freedom of action has been strongly affected by the territorial disputes with Venezuela. In this difficult situation, Guyana has been very adroit in its diplomatic moves. On the other hand, Jamaica's foreign policy is static it is limited to the consolidation of exist-

---

[42] See H.J. Maidenberg, "Venezuela and Brazil Fight for Influence over Guianas," *The New York Times,* 25 November 1968, pp. 69, 74.

ing relations with Britain and North America. Precautions are taken with regard to the possible entry of Britain into the European Economic Community. On the Caribbean scene, Jamaica has been extremely reluctant to join CARIFTA, while refusing to support a regional development bank located outside of Jamaica and by threatening to disrupt the functioning of existing common services, such as the University of the West Indies. As for Latin America, Jamaica has not yet undertaken any significant action.

6. Economists, lawyers, political scientists, and sociologists in the West Indies and in Latin America have to carry out substantial research to facilitate the task of policy-makers concerned with regional cooperation and integration. The main items on the agenda of a research programme could be the following:

A product-by-product analysis of potential trade relations;

Identification of possibilities for investment allocation, multinational enterprises, complementarity agreements, resource combination, and export substitution;

Coordination of development plans;

Establishment of regional financing and service institutions;

Compatibility of existing commitments with proposed arrangements, with particular reference to simultaneous affiliation with various integrative schemes;

Impact of political issues on a future economic partnership;

Importance of special bilateral relations (Jamaica-Mexico, Jamaica-Central America, Guyana-Brazil, Trinidad-Colombia, etc.), apart from overall regional schemes;

Position of Dutch-, French-, and Spanish-speaking Caribbean territories;

Restructuralization of economies in the light of a new economic partnership;

Relevance of the Central and South American experiences with integration to CARIFTA.

The Commonwealth Caribbean and Latin America find themselves at the threshold of a vast undertaking which will preoccupy an entire generation. Achievements made so far are embryonic and the difficulties which have already been identified contain promises of hard labour under tough conditions. There is no room for illusions and excessive enthusiasm. But there are sufficient elements to justify the expectation of reasonable, mutual benefits in the long run. The fact that results may not be overwhelming in the short-run does not allow for the postponement of action. On the contrary, the more distant benefits are, the sooner action is needed. Marshall Lyauthey one day complained to his gardener for having failed to plant a certain tree within a prescribed time limit. The gardener pointed out that it would take a hundred years for the tree to grow to full size, whereupon Lyauthey retorted: "That is exactly why the tree must be planted this afternoon."

THE FOREIGN TRADE AND TRADE POLICY OF THE ENGLISH-SPEAKING CARIBBEAN COUNTRIES

I. GROWTH PATTERN OF TRADE, 1950-1969

1. Introduction

Within the relative diversity of the countries in the geographical area of Latin America, those of the Caribbean have certain characteristics in common and have developed in a different socio-economic environment from the rest. The Caribbean countries obtained their political independence in comparatively recent years,[1] and it is only since then that they have enjoyed complete autonomy in the conduct of their trade relations, although for some years previously they had been gradually securing some measure of self-government in matters of internal policy and administration. Independence brought with it membership of the British Commonwealth, but this did not imply any substantive changes in the system of preferential trade relations established at the Economic Conference in Ottawa in 1932.

Thus, the growth pattern of the Caribbean countries' trade, both before and after their independence, has emerged within the institutional framework created by the agreements that have given shape to the British Commonwealth: in other words, the developing countries' role is essentially that of suppliers of primary commodities, in favour of which certain tariff and non-tariff concessions are granted, while in their turn they are required to grant preferential treatment to imports of industrial goods from the developed countries. Although the general economic policy of the Caribbean countries is directed towards tackling some of the problems common to all the developing countries (industrial development incentives, expansion and diversification of exports, higher growth rates for the domestic product, etc.), the measures and policies adopted have been such that the trade relations system inherited from the recent colonial past is left virtually intact. It must be recog-

nized, however, that the course of certain international events is forcing the Caribbean countries to face, at relatively short notice, the inevitable necessity of introducing substantive changes in their system of trade relations, both in order to avert possible clashes with policies aimed at speeding up economic development, and in order to make a full contribution to the establishment of a greater measure of fair play in trade between the developed and the developing countries.

2. Growth pattern of exports

The over-all annual growth rate of the Caribbean countries' aggregate exports averaged 8 per cent in 1950-1969. A breakdown by individual countries, however, reveals a very marked difference between the rate attained by Barbados, which was only 4 per cent annum, and the more satisfactory pace achieved by the other three countries. Similarly, the growth pattern of exports falls into two widely differing phases: in the case of Guyana, Jamaica, and Trinidad and Tobago, the rate of increase was highest from 1950-1952 to 1960-1962, and it declined sharply in the seven subsequent years, whereas for Barbados it was very low in the earlier period and improved in the later, when it slightly exceeded the figures for the other three countries (see table 1).

A salient feature in this group of countries is the high rate of growth attained by Jamaica's exports during the 1950s. At the beginning of the decade Jamaica started exporting bauxite and alumina, production of which expanded rapidly in the years that followed. While output of bauxite amounted to 1.2 million tons in 1953, by 1960 it had reached 5.8 million tons, and by 1969, 8 million. Such rapid development not only gave great dynamic impetus to the export sector, but considerably altered the composition of exports, more than 90 per cent of which had formerly consisted

[1] Jamaica and Trinidad and Tobago, in mid-1962; Barbados and Guyana, towards the end of 1966.

ECONOMIC BULLETIN FOR LATIN AMERICA (A United Nations Document), 1971, Vol. 1, pp. 104-116.

Table 1

CARIBBEAN COUNTRIES: AVERAGE VALUE OF TOTAL EXPORTS, 1950-1969

Country	Million of dollars			Percentage rates of increase		
	1950-1952	1960-1962	1967-1969	1960-1962 / 1950-1952	1967-1969 / 1960-1962	1967-1969 / 1950-1952
Barbados	20	26	39	2.6	5.9	4.0
Guyana	37	86	115	8.8	4.2	6.9
Jamaica	49	176	237	13.7	4.3	9.7
Trinidad and Tobago	121	326	458	10.4	5.0	8.1
Total, 4 countries	*227*	*614*	*849*	*10.5*	*4.7*	*8.0*

SOURCES: *Handbook of International Trade and Development Statistics* (United Nations publication, Sales No.: E/F.69.II.D.15); United Nations, *Monthly Bulletin of Statistics*.

of agricultural products. It also resulted in a change in the relative importance of external markets, since the country's high degree of dependence on the United Kingdom was lessened, and exports to Canada and the United States increased.

The favourable growth rate of exports from Trinidad and Tobago was also linked to one particular item—in this case, petroleum and petroleum products. It was attributable both to the expansion of domestic production and, more especially, to the practice of importing crude petroleum from Colombia and Venezuela for processing in local refineries. The difficulty of obtaining supplies from the Middle East during the Suez Canal crisis in 1956 created a very favourable opportunity for the expansion of exports from Trinidad and Tobago, as is apparent from the annual increase of 10.4 per cent recorded for the country's total exports in the 1950s. The slackening of this rate in the later years of the period under review reflects the more strenuous competition prevailing in the world market for petroleum products, which has even obliged some of the leading world exporters to regulate the expansion of production.

Export growth in Guyana, although slightly slower than in the two countries mentioned above, was also mainly concentrated in the earlier part of the period, and was due to increases in production of rice, sugar and bauxite. The negotiation of a regional rice agreement in 1956, under the terms of which Guyana became the principal supplier of rice in the Caribbean area, gave a considerable fillip to its rice exports at first, but in more recent years import requirements in some of the Caribbean countries and territories were reduced by the expansion of domestic production, so

that part of Guyana's rice exports were diverted to other markets. During the period 1962-1969, exports of rice, sugar and bauxite increased a good deal more slowly, with the result that the growth rate of total exports was lower than in the preceding ten years.

Of the Caribbean countries, Barbados showed the most sluggish export growth rate. From 1950-1952 to 1960-1962, this rate was only 2.6 per cent per annum, in sharp contrast with the position in the other three countries. The fact that sugar represents so high a proportion of Barbados' total exports (over 60 per cent in recent years) largely accounts for the unsatisfactory development of the country's external sector, since in the period mentioned there was no sign of an upward trend in sugar production. Between 1962 and 1969 total exports increased much faster, mainly by virtue of a vigorous upswing in re-exports and the emergence of certain new export lines. Some contribution was also made by the expansion of sugar exports resulting from the opening-up of the United States market, to which producers in the Caribbean area had not previously had access. The United States allocation of import quotas for sugar from the Caribbean countries not only enlarged these countries' export market but raised the average value of sugar exports, because price levels in the United States market were higher as a general rule than the prices laid down in the British Commonwealth's Sugar Agreement.

Broadly speaking, the conclusion may be reached that the growth pattern of total exports was a little more favourable in the Caribbean countries than in many others in the Latin American region, partly because of the preferential treatment accorded to the Caribbean countries in the United Kingdom market, and partly too because world demand for bauxite and petroleum products increased faster than demand for most agricultural commodities.

A glance at the composition of exports by staple products will show that their expansion was in fact essentially based on a few traditional items, and that only in recent years have a few new export lines begun to develop. The latter would seem to be the first fruits of certain export promotion measures that have been adopted, which will be discussed later.

The position of the Caribbean countries as regards the degree to which exports are concentrated in a few products is much the same as that of other countries in the Latin American area (see table 2).

The variations in the commodity exports concentration indexes are fairly small in most cases, probably because of the shortness of the period taken as the base for comparison and of occasional fluctuations in the share of certain commodities. At all events, it should be pointed out that, of the Caribbean countries, only in Barbados was there a relatively sharp drop in the concentration index, while the variations observed in the other three countries are only slight.

In the first place, it should be mentioned that, in Barbados, total exports have grown faster than exports of national products, that is, the share of re-exports has increased in recent years (see table 3).

Indeed, the proportion of re-exports in total exports increased from 14 per cent in 1958-1960 to 28 per cent in 1966-1968.

Unrefined sugar and molasses are the major national exports, though their share in the total has declined in recent years. In this connexion, it should be noted that sugar production in Barbados has undergone fairly wide fluctuations and has shown no definite growth tendency, so that the greater value of exports of those products in 1966-1968 (and even more so in the years immediately prior to 1966) is due principally to the greater unit value of exports to the United States, following the re-allocation to the Caribbean and other Latin American countries of the quota that was previously granted to Cuba. It is also interesting to note that the participation of Barbados in the British Commonwealth Sugar Agreement and its access to the United States market helped to prevent its sugar exports from suffering the effects of the sharp drop in sugar prices in the free trade area.

In recent years, Barbados has been able to develop some new exports; although these represent only a small proportion of the total, they signify the beginning of a greater diversification of exports. Particular mention may be made of crustacea and molluscs, lard and margarine, and some textile manufactures.

Guyana's exports are somewhat more diversified than Barbados', although in any case only three commodities (rice, sugar and bauxite) represent an average of 83 per cent of the total value of exports. The figures in table 3 show that rice exports grew fairly rapidly between the periods 1958-1960 and 1966-1968, while sugar exports remained at approximately the same level. In fact, the production of both

Table 2

LATIN AMERICA: COMMODITY EXPORTS CONCENTRATION INDEXES[a], 1960 AND 1966

Increase	1960	1966	Decrease	1960	1966
Guyana	54.3	55.4	Barbados	86.2	74.0
Cuba	76.6	86.4	Trinidad and Tobago	78.8	74.4
Ecuador	64.4	65.0	Jamaica	56.0	53.6
Panama	56.1	59.2	Colombia	74.3	66.4
Dominican Republic	54.1	59.8	Venezuela	72.5	70.2
Honduras	51.1	53.1	El Salvador	71.2	50.0
Nicaragua	46.0	51.7	Guatemala	69.4	49.6
Argentina	30.0	32.2	Costa Rica	60.9	46.2
			Brazil	58.0	46.3
			Mexico	27.2	24.3

SOURCE: UNCTAD, *Handbook of International Trade and Development Statistics* (United Nations publication, Sales No.: E/F.69.II.D.15), p. 143.
[a] The commodity concentration index is equal to 100 if only one commodity is exported, and its value decreases with the degree of diversification of exports. The formula used for calculation can be consulted in the source quoted.

Table 3

BARBADOS: TOTAL EXPORTS, BY MAJOR COMMODITIES

SITC Sections	Millions of dollars		Percentage of total	
	1958-1960	1966-1968	1958-1960	1966-1968
Over-all total	24.9	39.6	—	—
National exports	21.4	28.7	100.0	100.0
Section 0	19.5	24.7	91.1	86.1
Crustacea and molluscs	...	2.8	...	9.7
Raw sugar	16.4	18.6	76.6	64.1
Molasses	2.4	1.9	11.2	6.6
Lard and margarine	...	0.6	...	2.1
Section 1	1.3	1.8	6.1	6.3
Rum	1.3	1.7	6.1	5.9
Section 2	—	0.2	—	0.6
Section 3	—	0.3	—	0.9
Section 4	—	0.1	—	0.3
Section 5	0.5	0.3	2.3	0.9
Section 6	—	0.4	—	1.4
Section 7	—	0.3	—	0.9
Section 8	—	0.8	—	2.8

SOURCE: United Nations, *Yearbook of International Trade Statistics*, various issues.

rice and sugar reached a high rate of growth in the early 1950s, but while rice output continued to increase in the 1960s, the production of sugar suffered some setbacks, failing to rise above the figures recorded in previous years. Thus, the opening up of the United States market to Guyana's sugar exports (and the higher prices obtained on that market) served only to counteract the effects of the smaller volume of exports registered in the last few years. The value of sugar exports in 1966-1968 was thus approximately equal to their value in 1958-1960, but as in the same period the export value of other products increased, the share of sugar in the total value of exports declined from 49 to 28 per cent (see table 4).

The production of bauxite contributed most to the expansion of Guyana's exports. The average value of bauxite exports tripled in the course of the period concerned and their share in total exports rose from 23 to 42 per cent, ousting sugar from its place as the country's principal export item. The expansion of bauxite production and exports was due to the tariff and tax concessions accorded to foreign companies engaged in this activity. In the extractive industries sector, exports of manganese ore were initiated and diamond exports increased.

The changes in the respective share of the three most important commodities in Guyana's total exports, while not diminishing their proportion as a whole (83 per cent in 1958-1960 and 1966-1968), at least altered the structure of exports in favour of bauxite and other mining products, world demand for which, in general, has been more dynamic and has fluctuated less than demand for most agricultural commodities.

As stated previously, exports grew more rapidly in Jamaica than in any other Caribbean country, particularly in the 1950s. They are also more diversified, even though only three products—sugar, bananas and bauxite (including alumina)—supply the bulk of Jamaica's export earnings. Between 1958-1960 and 1966-1968, the value of exports of these three products increased in varying amounts, the largest increments being in bauxite and alumina; however, the share of sugar in the total decreased from 27 to 20 per cent, and that of bananas from 10 to 8 per cent. This was due, as indicated by the above figures, not to a decline in export values but rather to the faster growth of bauxite and alumina exports, which together accounted for about 48 per cent of total exports. The expansion of these exports has been stimulated by the various concessions accorded

Table 4
GUYANA: TOTAL EXPORTS, BY MAJOR COMMODITIES

SITC Sections	Millions of dollars		Percentage of total	
	1958-1960	1966-1968	1958-1960	1966-1968
Total	63.6	109.9		
National exports	62.7	106.8	100.0	100.0
Section 0	39.8	50.4	63.5	47.2
Crustacea and molluscs	...	4.0	...	3.7
Rice	6.4	14.0	10.2	13.1
Raw sugar	30.8	29.7	49.1	27.8
Molasses	...	2.1	...	2.0
Section 1	2.0	2.5	3.2	2.3
Rum	1.9	2.5	3.0	2.3
Section 2	17.7	49.6	28.2	46.4
Wood	1.6	1.7	2.6	1.6
Bauxite	14.6	45.0	23.3	42.1
Manganese	—	2.5	—	2.3
Section 3	—	—	—	—
Section 4	—	—	—	—
Section 5	0.7	0.8	1.1	0.7
Section 6	1.8	3.2	2.9	3.0
Diamonds	1.8	2.9	2.9	2.7
Section 7	0.3	—	0.5	—
Section 8	0.2	0.2	0.3	0.2

SOURCE: United Nations, *Yearbook of International Trade Statistics* (various issues).

to the companies controlling production and by the favourable trend of external demand. Preferential arrangements with the United Kingdom have guaranteed the access of agricultural products (sugar, bananas and citrus fruit) to that market at relatively stable prices. The unit sales value of bananas was raised by exporting them in cartons instead of stems. In contrast, coffee and cocoa exports were affected by a decline in production (see table 5).

The exports which have become most important in recent years are fuels, clothing and footwear, some chemical products and cement, all of which, although they represent fairly small proportions of the total value, have contributed to the diversification of Jamaica's exports.

Exports from Trinidad and Tobago consist mainly of petroleum and petroleum products, the share of agricultural products being the smallest in this group of countries. The growth of exports of petroleum and petroleum products is attributable partly to the development of domestic production, but mainly to imports of crude for local refining. In fact, while domes-

tic production of crude petroleum increased by 79 per cent between 1958 and 1968, imports of crude rose 241 per cent. The expansion of refining was favoured by the unstable conditions that have affected producers in the Middle East in certain years, and probably also by the more liberal treatment of foreign investment compared with other Latin American countries (see table 6).

Concurrently with the expansion of oil production and refining, Trinidad and Tobago has developed the production and export of some petrochemical products, which in 1966-1968 already represented 9 per cent of total exports. These, coupled with the increases recorded in exports of other manufactures, give Trinidad and Tobago's export sector a somewhat different character from that of other Caribbean countries, both because of the high proportion of petroleum products and because of the volume of manufactures whose share in total exports is larger than in any other Caribbean country.

The relatively small share of agricultural products, however, bears no relation to the importance of their production at the levels of

Table 5

JAMAICA: TOTAL EXPORTS, BY MAJOR COMMODITIES

SITC Section	Millions of dollars		Percentage of total	
	1958-1960	1966-1968	1958-1960	1966-1968
Total	144.5	229.3	—	—
National exports	138.0	220.7	100.0	100.0
Section 0	59.9	79.0	43.4	35.8
Raw sugar	37.6	44.4	27.3	20.1
Molasses	...	3.1	...	1.4
Bananas	13.7	17.5	9.9	7.9
Canned fruit	1.8	3.2	1.3	1.4
Fruit juices	2.3	2.9	1.7	1.3
Coffee	1.0	0.7	0.7	0.3
Cocoa	1.7	0.9	1.2	0.4
Section 1	5.4	6.8	3.9	3.1
Rum	3.5	2.9	2.5	1.3
Section 2	66.8	109.1	48.4	49.4
Bauxite	32.2	49.9	23.4	22.6
Alumina	32.8	57.6	23.8	26.1
Section 3	—	7.1	—	3.2
Section 4	—	—	—	—
Section 5	1.6	5.2	1.2	2.4
Section 6	1.5	3.2	1.1	1.4
Section 7	—	—	—	—
Section 8	2.4	10.0	1.7	4.5
Clothing	...	7.8	...	3.5

SOURCE: United Nations, *Yearbook of International Trade Statistics* (various issues).

Table 6

TRINIDAD AND TOBAGO: TOTAL EXPORTS, BY MAJOR COMMODITY

SITC Section	Millions of dollars		Percentage of total	
	1958-1960	1966-1968	1958-1960	1966-1968
Total	265.5	444.6	—	—
National exports	257.5	439.4	100.0	100.0
Section 0	31.4	34.5	12.2	7.9
Raw sugar	19.5	22.2	7.6	5.1
Molasses	—	1.6	—	0.4
Coffee	1.2	2.0	0.5	0.5
Cocoa	6.2	3.3	2.4	0.8
Fruit	3.3	3.7	1.3	0.8
Section 1	1.9	1.8	0.7	0.4
Rum	1.7	1.2	0.7	0.3
Section 2	2.7	2.8	1.0	0.6
Natural asphalt	1.2	1.9	0.5	0.4
Section 3	213.4	348.3	82.9	79.3
Section 4	0.2	0.2	—	—
Section 5	3.2	39.7	1.2	9.0
Ammonium compounds	—	15.6	—	3.6
Tar destillates	3.2	15.1	1.2	3.4
Ammonium sulphate	—	4.9	—	1.1
Section 6	3.0	4.6	1.2	1.0
Section 7	0.1	2.5	—	0.6
Section 8	1.5	4.4	0.6	1.0
Clothing	—	2.3	—	0.5

SOURCE: United Nations, *Yearbook of International Trade Statistics* (various issues).

income and domestic economic activities, oil production and refining and the chemical industry are highly capital-intensive activities employing a relatively small amount of manpower; hence, their rapid expansion has done little or nothing to solve the serious unemployment problem affecting about 20 per cent of the labour force. The sluggish growth of agricultural exports (production of which constitute the biggest source of employment) has not helped either to solve the unemployment problem.

3. Trend of imports

In every Caribbean country, the growth of imports between 1950-1952 and 1967-1969 followed roughly the same pattern as that of exports. As can be seen from table 7, in three of the countries (Guyana, Jamaica, and Trinidad and Tobago) the fastest-growing period was from 1950-1952 to 1960-1962, after which the rate of expansion showed a tendency to decline. Barbados' period of rapid growth, on the contrary, was between 1960-1962 and 1967-1969. Moreover, whereas Barbados' total imports grew considerably faster than its exports, the growth rate of imports was slightly lower than that of exports in the other three countries.

An important aspect of the general trend of imports in these countries is the extent of the changes in composition in terms of major categories of products. First of all, imports of food, beverages and tobacco are relatively high, particularly in Barbados, which has the region's least diversified agricultural sector. In Barbados, as in Guyana and Jamaica, these imports nonetheless expanded more slowly than those of other products and consequently accounted for a smaller percentage of the total

during the later years. Such was not the case in Trinidad and Tobago, where this particular group of products continued to make up around a quarter of the country's total imports. Although the reference periods for estimating the changes in the composition of imports are not very far apart and therefore cannot be expected to indicate any major modification, it would nevertheless seem fair to conclude that the import substitution policy for food products —one of the principal objectives of all the Caribbean countries' economic policy—has had somewhat meagre results.

Though they only make up a small percentage of the total, imports of crude materials and animal and vegetable oils and fats (SITC sections 2 and 4) have declined in relative importance throughout the Caribbean, except in Trinidad and Tobago.

Barbados and Guyana showed a tendency to increase the percentage of fuels and lubricants in their total imports, unlike Jamaica where the growth rate was much slower and represented a relative decline—partly because of the domestic production of petroleum, which has developed in recent years into an export product. Petroleum imports serve a different purpose in Trinidad and Tobago, being used not to satisfy domestic demand—as in the other countries—but to expand the capacity of local refineries to export petroleum products. The increase in these imports, from 32 per cent of the total in 1958-1960 to 51 per cent in 1966-1968, is clearly indicative of the growth of one of this country's industrial activities but does not have the same significance for countries where petroleum is for domestic consumption. It has therefore been left out of the present calculations, so as not to give a false picture of the percentage shares of all the other groups of products (see table 8).

Table 7

CARIBBEAN COUNTRIES: AVERAGE VALUE OF TOTAL IMPORTS

(Millions of dollars)

	1950-52	1960-62	1967-69	1960-62 / 1950-52	1967-69 / 1960-62	1967-69 / 1950-52
Barbados	28	49	87	5.8	8.5	6.9
Guyana	40	82	120	7.5	5.6	6.6
Jamaica	84	217	392	10.0	8.8	9.5
Trinidad and Tobago ..	123	329	438	10.4	4.2	7.8
Total	275	677	1,037	9.4	6.3	6.3

SOURCE: Handbook of International Trade and Development Statistics (United Nations publication, Sales No.: E/F.69.II.D.15); United Nations, Monthly Bulletin of Statistics.

68

Table 8

CARIBBEAN COUNTRIES: TOTAL IMPORTS, BY SITC SECTION

	Millions of dollars		Percentage of the total	
	1958-1960	1966-1968	1958-1960	1966-1968
Barbados				
Total	44.9	79.2	100.0	100.0
Foods, beverages and tobacco (sections 0 and 1)	13.8	20.8	30.7	26.3
Crude materials, oils and fats (sections 2 and 4)	2.6	3.4	5.8	4.3
Fuels and lubricants (section 3)	2.3	7.6	5.1	9.6
Chemicals (section 5)	3.4	6.0	7.6	7.6
Various manufactured goods (sections 6 and 8)	13.8	23.9	30.7	30.1
Machinery and transport equipment (section 7)	7.6	15.1	16.9	19.1
Other goods (section 9)	1.5	2.5	3.3	3.2
Guyana				
Total	72.9	118.8	100.0	100.0
Sections 0 and 1	14.5	19.9	19.9	16.7
Sections 2 and 4	1.4	2.0	1.9	1.6
Section 3	5.6	10.1	7.7	8.5
Section 5	5.6	11.1	7.7	9.3
Sections 6 and 8	26.2	38.4	35.9	32.3
Section 7	19.4	36.6	26.6	30.8
Section 9	0.3	0.6	0.4	0.5
Jamaica				
Total	196.7	353.5	100.0	100.0
Sections 0 and 1	44.3	71.7	22.5	20.3
Sections 2 and 4	8.9	12.1	4.5	3.4
Section 3	17.5	27.3	8.9	7.7
Section 5	16.1	28.5	8.2	8.1
Sections 6 and 8	66.0	121.2	33.6	34.3
Section 7	43.7	91.8	22.2	26.0
Section 9	0.3	0.6	0.2	0.2
Trinidad and Tobago				
Total	265.5	428.7		
Fuels (section 3)	86.0	218.8		
Total, excluding section 3	179.5	209.9	100.0	100.0
Sections 0 and 1	43.1	52.0	24.0	24.8
Sections 2 and 4	5.7	8.5	3.2	4.1
Section 5	12.5	20.2	7.0	9.6
Sections 6 and 8	68.7	72.4	38.3	34.5
Section 7	47.3	54.0	26.3	25.7
Section 9	2.1	2.6	1.2	1.2

SOURCE: United Nations, *Yearbook of International Trade Statistics* (several issues).

4. *Direction of trade*

To a large extent, the distribution of the Caribbean countries' trade among the major areas or countries of the world is the result of the traditional links they had with the United Kingdom prior to becoming independent. As members of the British Commonwealth, the Caribbean countries have free access to or preferential treatment in the United Kingdom market for their major exports and, in return, grant preferential treatment to imports from the United Kingdom. However, while the preferences granted by the United Kingdom are confined to agricultural products, those granted by the Caribbean countries apply to all imports. Because of this, the United Kingdom has held a dominant share in the foreign trade of the Caribbean countries, its relative share depending in each case on the proportion of agricultural exports in total exports. During the 1960s, however, there was a steady decline in the United Kingdom's share in the imports and exports of each of the Caribbean countries. With respect to exports, this decline was mainly attributable to the fact that the growth of exports was for the most part accounted for by mining products which either do not enjoy preferences or are exported to the country of origin of the company controlling production. With respect to imports, the decline is an indication that the preferential tariff has not always been the determining factor as regards origin, for its effects have been cancelled out or offset by other tariff concessions, for example special concessions covering imports of equipment, machinery and supplies for the installation of new industries or the expansion of existing industries.

In brief, it can be said that the most salient trend in Caribbean trade during the 1960s (as regards the origin and destination of imports and exports) has been the gradual erosion of the dominant position of the United Kingdom and the growth in the share of trade with the United States, which in some cases has taken over the United Kingdom's position as major trade partner. Moreover, the decline in the United Kingdom's position has been due, not to changes in its preferential trade with the Caribbean countries, but to the fact that their exports are growing and to the inflow of foreign investment (mainly from the United States) attracted by the concessions they offer.

Not surprisingly, Barbados' exports are the most concentrated in the United Kingdom market, owing to the large share of sugar exports and the preferential régime established under the British Commonwealth Sugar Agreement. In 1958-1960 the United Kingdom absorbed 60 per cent of Barbados' total exports, followed by Canada with 16 per cent. By 1966-1968, developments in the world sugar market had changed the distribution of exports, with the United Kingdom's share standing at 43 per cent of the total (although in absolute values exports to the United Kingdom remained unchanged) and Canada falling to third place with only 8 per cent. The decline in the share of these two countries, and the rise of the United States to the second most important market for Barbados' exports is attributable to the fact that Barbados, and other Caribbean countries, were given a United States sugar quota when all trade with Cuba was prohibited. Access to the United States market also meant that the sugar exports not covered by the British Commonwealth Sugar Agreement, which had formerly had to be sold either to United Kingdom or to Canada or to any other country at world free market prices, could be sold to the United States at prices much higher than those prevailing in the free market. Nevertheless, despite these changes in the relative share of the United Kingdom, the United States and Canada, total exports from Barbados continue to be concentrated virtually exclusively in these three countries, probably because they are so little diversified.[2] Although its exports to developing countries increased in absolute terms (virtually all to other Caribbean countries and territories), the share of such exports in the total declined slightly between 1958-1960 and 1966-1968 (see table 9).

The country distribution of Guyana's exports shows similar trends to that of Barbados. The United Kingdom (which absorbed 41 per cent of the total in 1958-1960) and Canada (29 per cent in 1958-1960) were relegated to second and third place, respectively, as a result of the sharp upswing in exports to the United States during the 1960s. in 1966-1968 the United States absorbed 24 per cent of total exports, while the United Kingdom and Canada accounted for 23 and 20 per cent respectively.

The rise of the United States to Guyana's major export market was due to some extent to the access to it of some of Guyana's sugar exports, but mainly to the expansion of the production of bauxite. Bauxite was also a contributory factor in the increase in the exports to other countries (Norway and Sweden in the European Free Trade Asociation, and the Netherlands and Italy in the European Economic Community); although this increase was not of great significance, it did at least constitute a break-through into new markets for Guyana's exports. The share of exports to developing countries, mainly in the Caribbean, rose from 14 per cent in 1958-1960 to 16 per cent in 1966-1968. This share consisted mainly of rice, Guyana having become a major rice supplier under an agreement between a number of Caribbean countries and territories.

The United States was already Jamaica's major export market in 1958-1960 (accounting for 29 per cent of total exports) and its

[2] These three countries absorbed 80 per cent of total exports in 1958-1960 and 64 per cent in 1966-1968, but in the latter period the proportion of exports not classified by destination was much higher (18 per cent).

Table 9

CARIBBEAN COUNTRIES: TOTAL EXPORTS BY MAJOR AREAS AND
COUNTRIES OF DESTINATION, 1958-1960 AND 1966-1968

	Millions of dollars		Percentage of the total	
	1958-1960	1966-1968	1958-1960	1966-1968
Barbados				
Total	25	40	100	100
Developed areas	20	26	80	65
Developing areas	5	7	20	18
Soviet areas	—	—	—	—
Unclassified[a]	—	7	—	18
United States	1	5	4	13
Canada	4	3	16	8
EEC countries	—	—	—	—
EFTA countries	15	17	60	43
United Kingdom	15	17	60	43
Japan	—	—	—	—
Latin America[b]	—	—	—	—
Guyana				
Total	63	110	100	100
Developed areas	53	86	84	78
Developing areas	9	18	14	16
Soviet areas	—	—	—	—
Unclassified[a]	1	5	2	4
United States	7	26	11	24
Canada	18	22	29	20
EEC countries	2	4	3	4
EFTA countries	26	32	41	29
United Kingdom	26	25	41	23
Japan	—	—	—	—
Latin America[b]	—	—	—	—
Jamaica				
Total	139	222	100	100
Developed Areas	134	204	96	92
Developing areas	5	14	4	6
Soviet areas	—	—	—	—
Unclassified[a]	—	3	—	1
United States	40	86	29	39
Canada	32	32	23	14
EEC countries	3	4	2	2
EFTA countries	58	80	42	36
United Kingdom	47	57	34	26
Japan	—	—	—	—
Latin America[b]	—	—	—	—
Trinidad and Tobago				
Total	258	444	100	100
Developed areas	170	335	66	75
Developing areas	53	74	21	17

71

Table 9 (*continued*)

	Millions of dollars		Percentage of the total	
	1958-1960	*1966-1968*	*1958-1960*	*1966-1968*
Soviet areas	—	—	—	—
Unclassified[a]	35	35	13	8
United States	47	188	18	42
Canada	13	18	5	4
EEC countries	23	26	9	6
EFTA countries	87	90	34	20
United Kingdom	77	54	30	12
Japan	—	—	—	—
Latin America[b]	12	9	5	2

SOURCE: International Monetary Fund and International Bank for Reconstruction and Development, *Direction of Trade. A Supplement to International Financial Statistics, Annual 1958-1962 and Annual 1964-1968.*
[a] Includes exports under the entry "Special categories" and also exports that could not be assigned to any area, mostly ships' bunkers, as noted in the above-mentioned source.
[b] Nineteen Latin American republics, not including Cuba, which the source places among the Soviet bloc countries.

share rose steadily to reach 39 per cent in 1966-1968. The reasons for this were similar to those in Barbados and Guyana, namely access to the United States market for part of its sugar exports and increased production and exports of bauxite and alumina. Another contributory factor, although of less importance, was the increase in Jamaica's exports of textile manufactures. During the same period the United Kingdom's share of exports fell from 34 to 26 per cent and Canada's from 23 to 14 per cent. Exports to other European countries (chiefly the other members of EFTA) increased their share in the total, which rose from 8 per cent in 1958-1960 to 10 per cent in 1966-1968. Exports to the EEC countries, however, remained at negligible levels. Lastly, it should be noted that the proportion of Jamaica's exports going to developing countries was the lowest of all the Caribbean countries.

Although the structure of Trinidad and Tobago's exports is fundamentally different from that of the other Caribbean countries, because of the large share of petroleum and petroleum products, the country distribution of its exports changed in similar fashion. The value of its exports to the United States rose from 47 to 188 million dollars between 1958-1960 and 1966-1968 (18 and 42 per cent of the total, respectively) making the United States its most important export market. Most of the increment was attributable to petroleum products and products of the petrochemical industry (chiefly fertilizers) and to certain manufactures produced by subsidiaries of United States companies. As in the other Caribbean countries, but much more markedly so, the share of the United Kingdom in Trinidad and Tobago's exports fell from 30 to 12 per cent, this being the only case in which exports to the United Kingdom fell in absolute terms. Petroleum and petroleum products do not receive preferential treatment in the United Kingdom, and hence Trinidad and Tobago does not have the same degree of market access to the United Kingdom as the other Caribbean countries, whose exports are composed mainly of agricultural commodities. Sugar, Trinidad and Tobago's major agricultural export, accounted for only 5 per cent of total exports in 1966-1968.

The decline in exports to the United Kingdom was, however, offset by the increase in exports to other members of EFTA, whose share in total exports increased from 4 to 8 per cent.

Trinidad and Tobago is the only Caribbean country whose exports to the EEC countries are of any significance, although they have fluctuated quite considerably. Although they rose slightly in value during the period considered, their share fell from 9 to 6 per cent. Exports to Canada followed a similar trend;

sugar being the major export, they were partially diverted to the United States market. Although sugar exports to Canada do not receive preferential treatment, in 1967 Canada agreed to return part of the import duties applied to Caribbean importers but, owing to the low price of sugar in the free market, this was not sufficient to counteract the high price on the United States market.

A feature common to all the Caribbean countries is the absence of export flows to the socialist countries. Similarly, export trade to Japan has been only very occasional and in virtually insignificant amounts. The situation is not the same, however, with the Latin American countries. Trinidad and Tobago is the only country with a steady export trade with certain Latin American countries, an average value of 12 million dollars in 1958-1960 which fell to 9 million in 1966-1968. The major market was Brazil, followed by Argentina and Venezuela. In recent years, Jamaica has exported some low-value items to Honduras.

With respect to imports, the most striking feature, as noted above, is the growing importance of imports from the United States. The most marked increase, in both absolute and relative terms, has been in imports by Guyana and Jamaica, where the expansion of bauxite and alumina production was financed by fresh United States investment. In Barbados and Trinidad and Tobago the rate of growth of imports from the United States was comparatively lower but still sufficient to raise the United States share in total imports (see table 10).

The growth of imports from the United States was accompanied by a decline in the share of imports from the United Kingdom, although only in the case of Trinidad and Tobago was there a decline in the value of United Kingdom imports. Considering that all the Caribbean countries have a fairly high margin of preference in favour of the United Kingdom, this decline in the United Kingdom's share demonstrates that preferential tariff concessions may be of only relative value if they are offset by other factors, for example differences in price, quality or the other cost components of imports, or tariff exemptions on imports of machinery, equipment and supplies for the installation of new import-saving or export-oriented industries. In all the Caribbean countries, the incentives offered to foreign investment have played an important role in the expansion of certain primary and manufactur-

ing activities and in the promotion of the tourist industry, and this in turn stimulated a greater flow of imports from the countries (principally the United States and Canada) supplying the investment.

Imports from the EEC countries account for a larger share of the total than exports to them, in Barbados and Guyana they grew at a rate comparable with that of total imports, while in Jamaica and Trinidad and Tobago they grew much more slowly, especially in Trinidad and Tobago where their absolute value slightly declined.

The trend of imports from Latin America was more favourable than that of exports to it. While Trinidad and Tobago was the only Caribbean country exporting to other Latin American countries, with the share of such exports falling from 5 per cent in 1958-1960 to 2 per cent in 1966-1968, imports from the Latin American countries increased substantially in Barbados, Jamaica, and Trinidad and Tobago. In the case of Trinidad and Tobago, this increase was virtually all due to increased purchases of crude petroleum from Venezuela and Colombia and is related to the expansion of plants refining petroleum for export. The scale of the increase in Trinidad and Tobago's imports of petroleum from these countries can be judged by the fact that their share in total imports rose from 25 per cent in 1958-1960 to 42 per cent in 1966-1968. Over the same period, the share of imports from Latin American countries in the total increased from 2 to 9 per cent in Barbados and from 2 to 7 per cent in Jamaica, this being due in both cases, as in Trinidad and Tobago, to increased imports from Venezuela.

The formation of the Caribbean Free-Trade Association (CARIFTA), as a result of the agreement that entered into force on 1 May 1968, boosted reciprocal trade among the Caribbean countries. The application of the first two sections of the automatic liberalization programme established in the agreement (a 20 per cent reduction in tariffs by May 1969, and a further 20 per cent by May 1970) has certainly been an important factor in the growth of intra-Caribbean trade. Between 1967 and 1969, imports from other Caribbean countries had risen by 50 per cent in Barbados, 31 per cent in Jamaica, 23 per cent in Trinidad and Tobago and 14 per cent in Guyana. In absolute terms, however, reciprocal trade among the Caribbean countries is still at an insignificant level and future growth will be hampered by the lack of diversification.

73

Table 10

CARIBBEAN COUNTRIES: TOTAL IMPORTS BY MAJOR AREAS AND
COUNTRY OF ORIGIN, 1958-1960 AND 1966-1968

	Millions of dollars		Percentage of the total	
	1958-1960	1966-1968	1958-1960	1966-1968
Barbados				
Total	45	79	100	100
Developed areas	35	62	78	78
Developing areas	9	17	20	22
Soviet areas	—	—	—	—
Unclassified	—	—	—	—
United States	5	10	11	13
Canada	6	7	13	9
EEC countries	4	7	9	9
EFTA countries	18	24	40	30
United Kingdom	17	23	38	29
Japan	1	1	2	1
Latin America	1	7	2	9
Guyana				
Total	73	119	100	100
Developed areas	60	98	82	82
Developing areas	12	19	16	16
Soviet areas	1	1	1	1
Unclassified	—	1	—	1
United States	12	30	16	25
Canada	6	12	8	10
EEC countries	7	13	10	11
EFTA countries	31	36	42	30
United Kingdom	31	35	42	29
Japan	1	4	1	3
Latin America	—	—	—	—
Jamaica				
Total	196	351	100	100
Developed areas	167	306	85	87
Developing areas	26	41	13	12
Soviet areas	1	—	—	—
Unclassified	2	3	1	1
United States	44	133	22	38
Canada	21	37	11	11
EEC countries	24	34	12	10
EFTA countries	72	80	37	23
United Kingdom	71	73	36	21
Japan	4	9	2	3
Latin America	4	23	2	7
Trinidad and Tobago				
Total	264	429	100	100
Developed areas	158	190	60	44
Developing areas	94	233	36	54
Soviet areas	1	—	—	—
Unclassified	11	6	4	1
United States	36	64	14	15
Canada	16	22	6	5
EEC countries	19	16	7	4
EFTA countries	86	71	33	17
United Kingdom	83	66	31	15
Japan	—	6	—	1
Latin America	65	179	25	42

SOURCE: As for table 9.

THE CARIBBEAN FREE TRADE ASSOCIATION: PROVISIONS AND IMPLICATIONS

Vincent R. McDonald

One of the principal obstacles to the development of the Caribbean[1] area has long been its inability to present a common marketing area as an incentive to would-be investors in the production of goods and services. As individual units, these territories have been faced with the diseconomies of production which are inherent in the absence of mass-production-type industries.

The per capita cost of establishing plants which are similar in their respective area is usually higher than that faced in more densely populated countries. The natural result is that this region has been faced with the unenviable choice of importing most manufactured goods and paying rather high prices or, on the other hand, seeing a plant established within its boundaries only to find itself paying equally high unit prices because of the diseconomies resulting from its inability to use its facilities at efficient output levels. Adding to this problem is the lack of a commitment by some industries to match increases in productivity by the labor force with matching wage increases [8].

THE REVIEW OF BLACK POLITICAL ECONOMY, 1971, Vol. 1, No. 3, pp. 65-77.

The repercussions from this phenomenon have long manifested themselves in that these territories have suffered from the absence of fully contributory investment and personal-consumption sectors. Rather, government and the foreign sectors (imports and exports outside of the Caribbean area) have shouldered the burden of the economy.

Another economic problem of this region is the lack of adequate transportation among the many countries. There is not enough adequate, fast, dependable intraregion transportation to meet the needs of maintaining production and distribution schedules. This condition results in an added burden being imposed on those goods that are traded, which also have to complete with goods produced, transported, and marketed by the more efficiently producing big-neighbor countries.

It is with this awareness that a number of Caribbean governments (Barbados, Guyana, the Leeward Islands,[2] Trinidad and Tobago, and the Windward Islands[3]) agreed in February, 1968, to cooperate by establishing a free-trade market area[4] – The Caribbean Free Trade Association – and signed the official document on April 30 1968, in Antigua.[5] Jamaica and Montserrat subsequently sought and received approval to enter into the agreement and did so in August, 1968. The result is that what started out with less than two million persons has now developed into a market area encompassing eleven governmental units and a diversified group of manufactured and agricultural economies of over four million persons, and it is projected to have more than five million persons by 1975 (Table 1).

These countries, which encompass an area of over 90,000 square miles, had a population density of 40,441 per square mile in 1960. This is projected to increase by 49 per cent to 60,081 by 1975, thereby adding substantially to the level of demand within the region (Table 1).

The purpose of this paper is to acknowledge the emergence of this trading bloc in the Caribbean and to explain its provisions and implications for regional cooperation and development.

ATTEMPTS AT COOPERATION

The merger of these economies for the purpose of economic integration[6] has not been the first attempt at

76

cooperation in this area. Perhaps the most famous of the original attempts is the West Indies Federation (1958-1962) whose collapse in part was probably due to the noncomplementarity of its members' economies. While the governments of the territories are well aware of the traditional insularities and nationalistic differences which permeate the region, the lack of cooperation among countries is not unique to this region. Carleen O'Loughlin points out:

> Federation as a form of government has not worked very well in emerging countries. It has been discussed or tried in the West Indies, in East Africa, in Central Africa, in Nigeria, in the Middle East, and in the Far East, and has resulted in complete failure or only limited success in every case although the reasons for failure are usually different. Even in the older federations of Australia, the United States and Canada, stresses imposed by this system of government are severe and often can only be overcome by conventional methods based on long experience.[6].

So, like the Latin American Free Trade Association (L.A.F.T.A.),[7] the European Free Trade Association (E.F.T.A.),[8] and to some extent the Central American Common Market (CACM),[9] the Caribbean Free Trade Association has, by the dropping of trade barriers (custom duties and quantitative restrictions), created a unified market for the trading of those products which originate in the area. Under this agreement, each signatory member still maintains its tariffs and other trade restrictions against nonmember countries. The justification for economic integration in the Caribbean is the same as that applied to integration by other groups of countries. Its intent is to serve as a catalyst of a sustained development effort within the shortest time possible via the expected benefits of economies of scale and specialization.

Concomitant to the rationale of the members is the hope for full employment, increased level of living, and optimum utilization of the available human and physical resources of the area.

> The preamble of the agreement states in part: Sharing a common determination to fulfill within the shortest possible time the hopes and aspirations of their peoples and of the peoples of other Caribbean countries for full employment and improved living standards...Conscious that their goals can most rapidly be attained by the optimum use of available human and

TABLE 1

Estimates of Population, Density, and Land Area of the West Indies
by Territories, 1960, and Projection 1965-1975

Territory	Area (Sq. Mi.)	Density	Census Pop. 1960	Projection 1965	Projection 1970	Projection 1975
Barbados	166	1,398	232,085	256,610	283,710	312,370
Jamaica	4,411	366	1,613,148	1,827,300	2,069,900	2,343,600
Trinidad and Tobago	1,982	418	827,957	948,660	1,087,200	1,245,700
Windward Islands	824	382	314,649	365,980	425,710	495,190
Leeward Islands	354	347	122,920	138,350	155,770	175,370
Guyana	83,000	7	558,769	649,950	756,010	874,380
Total	90,737		3,669,528	4,186,850	4,778,300	5,451,610
Density			40,441	46,143	52,661	60,081

Source: [9, p. 21].

TABLE 2

Estimated Growth of the West Indies Economies
with Projections through 1975 — In Millions

	1965 Total	1965 Per Capita	1970 Total	1970 Per Capita	1975 Total	1975 Per Capita
	BWI $	BWI $	BWI $	BWI $	BWI $	BWI $
Consumption by persons:						
Jamaica	1,036	595	1,319	701	1,564	763
Trinidad and Tobago	801	840	1,014	924	1,223	968
Leeward Islands, Windward Islands, Barbados	256	355	310	401	368	443
Guyana	228	352	264	354	305	355
Total	2,321	571	2,907	646	3,460	692
National income:						
Jamaica	1,199	686	1,530	811	1,855	907
Trinidad and Tobago	988	1,436	1,251	1,141	1,499	1,186
Leeward Islands, Windward Islands, Barbados	278	386	340	440	418	503
Guyana	285	441	328	441	377	439
Total	2,750	676	3,449	766	4,149	830
Gross domestic product at factor cost:						
Jamaica	1,365	782	1,732	917	1,910	935
Trinidad and Tobago	1,229	1,289	1,558	1,420	1,861	1,473
Leeward Islands, Windward Islands, Barbados	293	404	357	460	438	527
Guyana	322	299	372	499	427	497
Total	3,207	789	4,019	892	4,636	928

BWI $1 = U.S. $0.583

Source: [9, p. 11].

other resources...Aware that the broadening of domestic markets through the elimination of barriers to trade between the territories is a prerequisite for development and convinced that such elimination of barriers to trade can best be achieved by the immediate establishment of a Free Trade Area and the ultimate creation of a Customs Union and a viable Economic Community we hereby set the following objectives:

a. To promote the expansion and diversification of trade in the area of the Association.
b. To encourage a balanced and progressive development of the economies of the area.
c. To ensure that trade between member territories takes place under conditions of fair competition.
d. To foster the harmonious development of Caribbean trade and its liberation by the removal of barriers, and
e. To ensure that the benefits of free trade are equitably distributed among the member nations [1].

To achieve these objectives, CARIFTA has established tariff reductions with gradual elimination clauses among the member nations.

The Arrangements

The potential growth of the economies of the members of CARIFTA is seen in Table 2. The projections over the five year period 1970-1975 estimate a growth of 18.4, 20.5, and 15.3 per cents in the levels of consumption, national income, and gross domestic product, respectively. The extent to which these estimates are achieved will determine the pace at which CARIFTA will achieve its stated goals.

Reserve List

In an effort to minimize the difficulties of transition to the free-trade commitment and because of the marked variation in the level of development of the respective economies (see Table 2), recognition was given to the problems of the smaller, less developed members of the association. A reserve list — a list of commodities on which import duties are not removed immediately — was established. This arrangement allows the smaller countries an extended period in which to

79

adjust their industries to a free-trade status [1].

The reserve list is included in Annexes B and D of the consolidated text of the Agreement. It allows that duties be gradually removed over a five-year period for the four larger and more developed countries (Barbados, Guyana, Jamaica, and Trinidad and Tobago) and over ten years for the less developed countries of the Leeward and Windward Islands [1]. j The rationale given for this action – the gradual elimination of import duties – is an attempt to minimize sharp dislocations of production in a member country as a result of a sudden increase in competition from a more efficient industry located in another member country. Additionally, this step averts a sudden loss of revenue resulting from the abrupt removal of import duties on a commodity which prior to free trade was a primary source of revenue for the member country.

A number of items have been placed on a reserve list. Annex B includes two categories of products. In one category there are some thirteen items from which the less developed and the more developed countries must remove duties in ten and five years, respectively. The products in the first category are: preserved fruits and fruit preparations, unmanufactured tobacco; prepared paints, enamels, lacquer, and varnishes; detergents; crates and wooden containers; radio and television sets; accumulators, wood and metal furniture; mattresses; underwear and shirts of knitted fabrics and underwear shirts and nightwear of fabrics other than knitted; leather slippers and house footwear; and leather footwear [4].

Those in the second category are: biscuits, coir products; mats and matting; brushes made of plastic except paint and artists' brushes [4].

Revenue Provisions

In addition, Annex D deals with the question of revenue from the reserve list. Two categories of goods are included here – alcoholic beverages and petroleum products. All countries are required to remove the "effective protective element" in revenue duties over a five-year period in regad.to the above group of goods. In this case, the protective element in revenue duty is considered to be the difference between the import duty and the excise duty, which requires then that the domestically produced goods and the same goods imported from a CARIFTA country must have equal treatment in tax assessments at the end of the transition period.

Other Provisions

Many difficulties the countries will face in administering the provisions of the Agreement are recognized. For example, Article 3 recognizes the existence of prior special agreements which the parties had subscribed to before the Association. Each member is required to reconcile the provisions of any such agreements with the purposes of this agreement.

Article 5 imposes an "origin test." That is, the exporting country must adhere to the principle that the product was completely produced within the area, using the "appropriate qualifying process," and that value of any materials imported from outside the area does not exceed 50 per cent of the export price of the goods.

Provision for the imposition of nondiscriminatory purchase taxes (Article 7) and provision for the gradual phasing out of export duties (Article 9) are spelled out. While the member territories are prohibited from applying export duties, they are still free to take any measures necessary to prevent evasion of duties through the reexporting of commodities via an Association member. While there are no quantitative import or export restrictions (Articles 13 and 14), the Agreement provides the machinery for dealing with the problem of dumping whether practiced by one CARIFTA country against another or by an outside country. In either situation, member countries are expected to act in accordance with their international obligations under the GATT agreements which have provisions for dealing with dumping.

Agricultural Marketing Agreements

The concern of the Association with the marketing of agricultural products reflects the fact that the countries involved are and have been agrarian by nature. Inroads have been made in introducing mechanization in a number of the agricultural industries, but this has not contributed substantially to reducing the ills of the region. E. Gordon Erickson says: "Mechanization results in producing a higher yield per man employed, not an appreciably higher yield per acre cultivated...Mechanization is essential in such countries as the United States where labor is relatively scarce and expensive. But in the West Indies the conditions are just the reverse. There is a plethora of labor and a lack of full employment [2]."

While the plantation form of agricultural organization which was predominant in the region (sugar, bananas, coffee, rice) for centuries has diminished, the continual demand for agricultural products to satisfy domestic consumption and indirectly aid the search for foreign exchange through the satisfying of hotel needs (a vibrant growth area in most of the member countries) continues.[10]

In practice, there is little if any import duty on agricultural foodstuffs. The governments agreed on a list of products which would be subject to free trade among member territories. In an effort to encourage agricultural production in the region, the members agreed on the restriction of agricultural imports from extraregional sources unless they could not be supplied by a member country.

This agreement, which is quite similar to the Oils and Fats Agreement, allows the Regional Secretariat, upon notification by the member territory of its shortage or surplus of a commodity, to allocate the markets for the particular products based on the proportion of their import or export availability to the area.[11]

The protocol encompasses the following commodities: carrots, peanuts, tomatoes, red kidney beans, black pepper, sweet peppers, garlic onions, potatoes (not sweet), potatoes (sweet), string beans, cinnamon, cloves, cabbage, plantains, pork and pork products, poultry and meat, eggs, okra, fresh oranges, pineapples, and pigeon (congo) peas.

Subsumed within the provisions established for agricultural production is the expectation that eventually the general development of agricultural commodities in the member countries of CARIFTA should be coordinated. Pending this arrangement, member countries may impose quantitative restrictions on imports from other CARIFTA countries included in the Agricultural Marketing Protocol or give government aids (such as subsidies and price guarantees) to their domestic agricultural production in order to develop their agriculture.

The significance of agricultural production is paramount. In a recent report it was found that the value of domestic agricultural production in Jamaica in 1968 was $23.2 million. At the same time the country imported $32.4 million of food while exporting $32 million of agricultural products. This represents aggregate agricultural transactions of $87.6 million with more than 35 per cent of its needs being imported. [7] In fact there are reports that the expenditures for food by hotels, also a vital part of each country's economy, result in up to 80 cents out of every dollar leaving the region for agricultural imports.

IMPLICATIONS

The Caribbean free-trade area is now in effect. The formal legal documents have been promulgated and the indications are that the level of trade among these countries will be well in excess of previous levels.

Naturally, there are questions as to whether this economic merger will serve as the precursor of economic development for the region and whether the major beneficiaries will be the large countries (Jamaica, Trinidad and Tobago, Guyana and Barbados) or the smaller islands.

Most proponents of economic integration have recognized that the benefits from this form of cooperation cannot be achieved unless political integration is pursued and achieved also. In practice, economic integration is but a routine phenomenon but political integration is much more mercurial.

True viable economic integration cannot be accomplished without political accord. Problems such as wage and price differentials, freedom of movement, regional banking and currency can only be adequately dealt with if there is political cooperation. In the absence of political integration the institutions designed to achieve economic integration will falter regardless of the wellfounded intentions of the participants. Such failure will not be a result of the structure or goals of the group but of the absence of a mutual climate of trust and understanding for their implementation.

Answers to the impact of this bloc in the Caribbean are still inconclusive. However, it is clear that while this is a relatively weak form of integration, it is the most significant innovation in Caribbean maneuvering since the collapse of the West Indies Federation in 1962. The past failures continue to haunt the leaders and people of the region, and the current feeling is that the birth of CARIFTA will forge the region into a strong, viable economic bloc in the current decade. The converse of this situation is that of the breakdown of this agreement with the resulting disillusionment of an already restless, growing populace.

Of these contrasting alternatives, the former is foreseen on a conditional basis. The wind of change which has been blowing in this area has lent credence to the idea that economic gains are possible through cooperation and the enlargement of the market area. The next step — some level of political cooperation — must be pursued and achieved in conjunction with efforts being made to improve the region economically. A unified far-sighted regional plan must be arrived at encompassing both economic and political questions, with its emphasis on nationals becoming more involved in the production of goods and services and in the ownership of the economic resources of the region. As long as such cooperation is lacking the region will suffer from the paradox of insularity — , what might be good for the individual countries in the short run could well turn out to be detrimental to the whole region in the long run.

Hopes of the probable success of this venture are strengthened by the report that the government of the Dominican Republic has taken under advisement the making of a formal application for membership in the association. What this would mean is that the marketing area and its population would be doubled. Naturally, there are spill-offs in terms of economies of scale from producing for this much larger market area.

An additional factor suggesting the probable success of this venture is the recent establishment of a regional development bank, headed by the well-respected West Indian economist, Professor W. Arthur Lewis. The bank, which has support from the United States, Canada, and Britain, will provide a source of capital which has so far been unavailable. At the very least, the presence of this bank should provide the confidence and sustenance for the smaller countries in the area. They came into CARIFTA without the infrastructure of their larger colleagues; with an adequate source of reasonable, available capital, they can join the race toward development. This, coupled with the fact that three of the four independent countries (Jamaica, Barbados, Trinidad and Tobago) have become members of the Organization of American States (OAS) and the other, Guyana, which became a republic in February, 1970, is also likely to become a member as soon as it is able to reconcile its border differences with Venezuela and Surinam, provides added incentive for the governments to cooperate with each other.

The economic opportunities which are available in this region have not been relegated to local investors. In fact, it is unfortunate that the major reliance has been on foreign investors. The point is not to bar foreign investors; in fact, the feeling is that they should be encouraged to continue investing in this region in even larger amounts. The point is that the respective governments in the region must institute policies which allow such investors to operate on a more competitive basis than one based on "certainty of profits."- Some mechanism must be instituted in each country if not on a regional basis for the recycling of profits. Industries such as bauxite, petroleum, and banking must provide greater equity interest to local governments.

The fact that the individual countries do not have enough capital to accomplish unilaterally the required development of localized resources is a factor in favor of such joint cooperation. In addition, a policy seeking the pooling of local capital must be encouraged[12] and rewarded, but for CARIFTA to succeed some external capital must be injected into the region.

In spite of this belief, it should be clear to external investors that the introduction of foreign personnel and capital into this area must be done on guidelines established by the national governments with provisions for an equitable sharing of the returns within the country. Under such conditions it is important that foreign investors recognize this obligation on the part of the respective governments and do not interpret such actions as being anti-investor. It is only on terms of true partnership that the mutual interests of economic development and national self-respect can be determined. Under such agreements external investors can contribute or should be allowed to contribute to the development of this area.

1. The Caribbean is defined here as those islands and countries which are contiguous to the Caribbean Sea. It is projected to have more than 5 million persons by 1975 (Table 1).

2. Antigua, St. Kitts, Nevis, Anguilla, Montserrat.

3. Dominica, Grenada, St. Lucia, St. Vincent.

4. A free-trade area is but one of many forms which economic integration might take. As Ingo Walter and Hans C. Vitzthum point out in [10], "Economic integration can take a variety of forms, ranging from loose intergovernmental agreements to liberalized international trade and productive factor movements to the complete fusion of two or more national economies into a single, unified multinational economic entity, complete with supranational institutions."

5. Actually, the principal agreement establishing the Association was initially signed at Dickenson Bay, Antigua, on Dec. 15, 1965, by the Chief Minister of Antigua, V. C. Bird, and the Premiers of Barbados, E. W. Barrow, and of British guiana, L. F. S. Burnham [4, p. 3].

6. Economic integration takes several forms. It might consist of complete economic integration, where there is a total assimilation of the institutions of the cooperating countries; the establishment of a common market in which restrictions on goods and factor products are abolished; a customs union where tariffs and quantitative restrictions are abolished between member countries; and/or a free-trade area with the addition of common trade restrictions against nonmember countries.

7. It includes Argentina, Bolivia, Brazil, Chile, Colombia, Ecuador, Mexico, Paraguay, Peru, Uruguay, and Venezuela.

8. It includes United Kingdom, Norway, Denmark, Sweden, Switzerland, Austria, and Portugal.

9. It includes Costa Rica, El Salvador, Guatemala, Honduras, Nicaragua.

10. In Jamaica, for example, agriculture — including forestry, fishing, and mining — in 1967 accounted for less than 25 per cent of the GDP and a similar pattern is seen in the other countries.

11. One difference from the Oils and Fats Agreement is that the member territory may export its products outside of the region before satisfying regional demand if it can get a higher price outside.

12. A recent recognition of this is the setting up of a Unit Trust (Jamaican Investment Fund) in Jamaica. It is an attempt to allow the general public to participate in the ownership of industry and commerce by investing their savings on their behalf. In addition, the government has approved special income-tax incentives for holders of units in the fund.

REFERENCES

[1] Caribbean Free Trade Association Agreement; Argument and Related Document *Appendix I, April, 1968.*

[2] *Ericksen, E. Gordon,* The West Indies Population Problem — Dimensions for Action *(Lawrence: University of Kansas, 1962).*

[3] *Gannun, Thomas A. (ed.),* Doing Business in Latin America *American Management Association (New York: 1968).*

[4] *Government of Trinidad and Tobago,* CARIFTA and the Caribbean Economic Community *(Government Printery,Trinidad, Trinidad and Tobago, 1968).*

[5] *Krause, Walter (ed.),* The Economy of Latin America, *(Iowa City: Bureau of Business and Economic Research, The University of Iowa, 1966).*

[6] *O'Loughlin, Carleen,* Economic and Political Change in the Leeward and Windward Islands, *(New Haven: Yale University Press, 1968).*

[7] The Daily Gleaner, *Feb. 25, 1970.*

[8] *Thomas, Clive, "Sugar Economics in a Colonial Situation; A Study of the Guyana Sugar Industry,"* Ratoon, Studies in Exploitation, *No. 1.*

[9] *United States Department of Agriculture,* Jamaica, Trinidad and Togabo, Leeward Islands, Windward Islands, Barbados and British Guiana, Projected Levels of Demand, Supply, and Imports of Agricultural Products to 1975 *(E.R.S. Foreign 94, Israel Program for Scientific Translations, Jerusalem, 1963).*

[10] *Walter, Ingo, and Hans C. Vitzthum,* The Central American Common Market, *(New York: N.Y.U. Graduate School of Business Administration, May, 1967). Bulletin No. 44.*

CARIBBEAN ECONOMIC INTEGRATION—PROBLEMS AND PERSPECTIVES

By HAVELOCK BREWSTER

I. INTRODUCTION

THREE analyses of the breakdown in 1962 of the West Indies Federation have appeared[1] at a time when new steps, the inauguration of the Caribbean Free Trade Association,[2] have been taken into regionalism. They are by persons who were closely involved with the Federation experience—Dr. Eric Williams, the Prime Minister of Trinidad & Tobago, Professor Gordon Lewis who was at one time a consultant to the Trinidadian Chief Minister and Sir John Mordecai who was the Deputy Governor-General of the Federation together with Sir Arthur Lewis who at times acted as an adviser. These analyses are conducted at different levels. Williams's seems to be restricted, more or less, to a re-assertion that the Jamaican and Trinidadian conceptions of Federation were basically irreconcilable, the former opting for a weak version and the latter for a strong one. Gordon Lewis, in addition to the usual political and economic issues, turns to sociological phenomena. He suggests that, in brief, there was a fatal ambiguity in the West Indian psychology, at least so far as 'middle class patriots' were concerned— passionate nationalism and uncritical acceptance of 'the British belief in the civilizing mission of British imperialism'. It followed then, according to this view, that the institutional forms of the Federation based upon that contradiction would be imperfect and unsatisfactory. In essence, his position is similar to that of Williams and it takes a view with respect to Jamaica which is less constructive than it is destructive. His stand seems to be that a more integrated conception of regionalism should have been put into effect in 1958 when the Federation was inaugurated but is effectively contradicted by the statement that it is all too easy 'to indulge the temptation of blaming individuals like Manley and Bustamante[3] instead of seeing that individuals reflect the social

---

[1] Eric Williams, *Inward Hunger—The Education of a Prime Minister*, Andre Deutsch, 1967; Gordon K. Lewis, *The Growth of the Modern West Indies*, MacGibbon & Kee, 1968, Chapters XIV, XV; John Mordecai, *The West Indies—The Federal Negotiations*, Allen & Unwin, 1968 (Epilogue by W. Arthur Lewis).

[2] *Agreement Establishing the Caribbean Free Trade Association*, Georgetown, Guyana, 1968. The Association embraces Jamaica, Barbados, Trinidad & Tobago, Guyana, Antigua, Montserrat, St. Kitts, Dominica, St. Lucia, Grenada.

[3] Mr. Norman Manley was then the Chief Minister of Jamaica and Mr. Alexander Bustamante the leader of the opposition party.

JOURNAL OF COMMON MARKET STUDIES, 1971, Vol. 9, No. 4, pp. 282-298.

pressures of their time (and) in this particular case, both the Jamaican leaders were merely the mouth-pieces for a Jamaican insularity'.

Mordecai assembles a mass of diplomatic and administrative detail which is of value as a record of the sort of day-to-day attitudes and occurrences to be encountered and avoided. One of the important points made by Mordecai and Arthur Lewis is that the leadership, in common with incipient radicalism, was lacking in maturity so far as the art of compromise is concerned. This is shown in two ways. The first was its failure to understand that the initial concentration, at least in a federal kind of arrangement, should have been on those things on which there was agreement. The second was that its pattern of communication often tended to be antagonistic and therefore ineffectual. There may be a lot of good sense in these views but questions remain and are posed now, though in a somewhat different context, about the kinds of short-run compromise which are possible that do not compromise longer-run objectives and, equally important, about the extent to which such possibilities are ultimately a matter for decision by the governments of Caribbean countries, given their small size and extreme openness.

2. FEDERATION AND INTEGRATION

A variety of reasons have been advanced to explain why these initial attempts at regionalism failed and it is unnecessary to repeat them here. It may be worthwhile, however, to take up one or two features which may have some bearing on the current situation. We have, first, the notion of a lack of popular participation, 'absence of public ripeness', as the British used to term it. It is fairly clear, however, that in the Eastern Caribbean the idea of West Indian integration never did command the kind of hostility which could raise it to the level of a pivoting issue in competitive party politics. In Jamaica itself, only 33 per cent of the electorate actually voted in the 1961 referendum against Federation and that after the opposition party in that country under Alexander Bustamante's leadership had made use of out-of-date arguments against the arrangement.[4]

The facts are, however, that the Federal issue did become in Jamaica 'a political football' and it contributed much to Manley's failure in the 1962 general elections. This situation is often attributed to a so-called insularity in that country and its separateness from the Eastern Caribbean.[5] However, another line of explanation suggests that political

---

[4] These arguments in general suggested that Jamaica would have to subsidize the smaller islands in one form or another, a matter which the Federal authorities had already agreed to dismiss as impracticable and not possible.

[5] Michael Manley, 'Overcoming Insularity in Jamaica', *Foreign Affairs*, October 1970.

89

party control in Jamaica, because of its elitist structure (middle-class patriots cum businessmen) tends to sublimate the really basic problems of life in that country and thereby to bring to the front a variety of issues (Federation, ganga, strikes, internal security, crime, communism, human rights and black power) which are removed in varying degrees from the harsher realities of the day. The point to consider is that as long as the composition of political parties is such that the competition in politics can be conducted substantially outside the arena of grass-roots issues, a threat will always be posed by the possibility of political manipulation of the population's responses—in Jamaica or elsewhere—to any current symbolic scape-goat such as regionalism.

A second feature is the idea that regionalism was something forced on West Indian people from outside, that is at the initiation of the British, and that this, as such, is an important contributing reason for its failure. The real question, however, is the sort of concepts decision-makers have been operating with. Thus, it may well be asked even now whether native decision-makers are not themselves in the grip of alien ideas serving systems based on substantially irrelevant experience.

In Federation, the issue from the start was conceptualized, or rather constitutionalized, as a struggle between central political authority and the constituent political units, so that the powers of the former are inversely related to those of the latter. Such an application of European political liberalism seems simplistic where the locus of power is affected by a dynamic complex of linkages and trade-offs between the control of decisions and economic strength. And so, too, the idea of economic integration has been formulated, essentially, as a curtailment of the power of the nation-state to impede competition in inter-State trade. Such a deduction from the premises of classical economics by-passes the fact that there is actually not much to compete in and that the 'rules of the game' are only operative to the extent that people want to apply them. The meaningful question at the present time for the Caribbean, as for most of the economic groupings in the less developed world, must be: how to promote trans-national economic development whilst minimizing infringement of State sovereignty.

Current experiences and their interpretations, particularly of the EEC, would suggest, at the general level, that economic–political spill-over is not as closely correlated or indiscriminate as regards the acts involved as used to be assumed in theory.[6] Also, in the context of individual, small, open States in the Carribbean the question arises as to how wide their degrees of freedom really are over otherwise vital concerns such as external and internal economic policy, military

---

[6] Cf. Stanley Hoffmann, 'The Fate of the Nation-State', *Daedalus*, 1966; Roger D. Hansen, 'Regional Integration—Reflections on a Decade of Theoretical Efforts', *World Politics*, 1968.

strength, defence arrangements and foreign policy and therefore about their ability to take and implement significantly mutually divergent decisions. Another factor lessening supranational implications of economic decisions is the (unexplored) possibility of under-politicization in several economic integration issues, for example internal agricultural policies, transport policy, regional currencies, transnational migration, common external tariffs, foreign economic relations, external monetary policy. It is interesting to consider that this may exist side by side with over-politicization[7] in certain other issues; for example, differences in the rates of growth of intra-regional trade.

If, however, the degree of inter-state divergence in central economic and political policy is effectively limited by hemispheric parameters, and thereby also the true potential significance of supranational legislation developing from transnational economic decisions, its corollary of conformity to internationalized norms poses problems of relevance. For example, in the Caribbean there is a tendency for activity, even nation-states, to be conceived as a matter of 'writing out the constitution', rather than as a matter of objectives and functions. This was absurdly true of the Federation as it was also of the Caribbean Free Trade Association (CARIFTA). Practically every meeting on federation since the 1920s began with the participants getting down to 'drafting the constitution'. And CARIFTA was literally a transcription of the European Free Trade Association Treaty, including its errors.

Another internationalized concept, 'gradualism', inspires this kind of unreality, with the imagery of confidence and maturity. To deal with questions suggested by the thesis of gradual progression obviously calls in the first place for discrimination between various kinds of action and commitment. It cannot be presumed that the idea of gradual and continuous progress is applicable at all times to all possible kinds of initiative in all possible kinds of circumstances. And the point may equally well be made about political as about economic integration. For example, the groupings in East, West and Central Africa, the League of Arab States, the Latin American Free Trade Association and even the Central American Common Market do not provide at the present time convincing evidence of the operation of an internal dynamic for gradual and continuous progress even within the restricted area of regional economic cohesiveness. This may be of some significance to CARIFTA considering that, in addition to this negative inter-regional experience of gradualism, it does not have the stimulus of initial built-in commitments beyond the freeing of trade barriers.

7 J. S. Nye, Jr., 'Patterns and Catalysts in Regional Integration', *International Organization*, XIX, Autumn 1965; Hansen, op. cit.

3. TARIFF LIBERALIZATION AND PRODUCTION INTEGRATION

The new moves toward integration in the Caribbean have involved differences of opinion about the role of trade liberalization in regional development. The contrasting approaches are the 'phased freeing of trade' and 'production integration'. The latter, mainly outside the Anglo-Saxon world, has challenged in recent years, the traditional (Vinerian) theory of customs union as a theory of integration, particularly as it concerns less-developed countries.[8]

The argument supported here is that the trade liberalization approach of itself could have only a minor impact and moreover, as a technique for promoting regional co-operation,' may have a negative result. To begin with, intra-West Indian trade is very small—6 per cent of the total trade which is equivalent to 3 per cent of the GDP—and 75 per cent of it is taken up by two products, rice from Guyana and petroleum from Trinidad. In addition, the general incidence of the tariff was very low (in contrast to the Latin American situation), being less than 15 per cent whilst the other elements of competition were highly imperfect.

The price effect, therefore, of tariff reductions would necessarily be very small though this could be improved by direct promotional activity. Given the high import-content of manufactures, such increases of trade as might take place in these products would have a limited effect on the GDP. The fact that tariffs were already quite low by international standards gives rise to some doubt that a West Indian notional margin of preference of 10–15 per cent could have any substantial impact on the relative share of intra-West Indian trade in manufactures. A great many manufactured products, particularly in the Eastern Caribbean, carried such low tariffs that their elimination could scarcely have any real effect on West Indian competitiveness in relation to third-country suppliers. Moreover, when one takes into account the high import content of these goods the effective margin of preference is reduced to the low level of 2–3 per cent. Further, it is questionable whether member countries like Guyana and Barbados acted wisely in giving up the *right* to offer protection to *non-existent* industries which, on the basis of the experience in Trinidad and Jamaica, might be feasible on a national scale.

It is also clear that barriers to agricultural trade were not really an

[8] Cf. Francois Perroux, 'L'Intégration et L'Echec de la Théorie Traditionnelle des Echanges Extérieurs', *Economie Appliquée*, Vol. XXI, 1968; Gérard Destanne de Bernis, 'Les Industries, Industrialisantes et L'Intégration Economique Régionale', *Economie Appliquée*, 1968; Imre Vajda, 'Integration, Economic Union and the Nation State', *The New Hungarian Quarterly*, Vol. IX, No. 31, Autumn 1968; Hiroshi Kitamura, 'Economic Theory and Regional Economic Integration of Asia', *The Pakistan Development Review*, Winter 1962; Havelock Brewster and Clive Y. Thomas, 'El Liberalismo Economico y El Concepto de Integracion', *Foro Internacional*, No. 36, August 1969.

important matter since they were very low and in many cases, particularly in the Leeward and Windward Islands and Trinidad, were already nil. Nor was there any evidence to suggest that it was trade barriers which were impeding trade in agricultural products. And finally, the Leeward and Windward Islands derive the greater portion of their revenue from customs duties whilst at the same time the prospects for increasing income from import substitution are very doubtful on account of their minute size.

A set of institutional dangers follow. Firstly, the matter of trade barrier removal may become a substantive subject involving in it a bureaucratic machinery to contend with a complex of administrative, legal and political affairs surrounding what in essence is not a very productive issue. Secondly, this approach lends itself, as the experience in East Africa and Central America shows, to the idea that the relative increase in trade which each of the units secure with each other is a measure from the standpoint of individual states of the success or failure of these moves to integration. Thus again the likelihood arises of a considerable amount of initiative being devoted to an issue which is substantially false, with the concomitant political and commercial controversies which it gives rise to. Thirdly, the possibility is present that no advance into new and more creative dimensions of co-operation would take place: the apparatus of trade liberalization would absorb the whole commercial and official disposition to co-operation. The pace of advance would be set by the States which are least inclined to regional development, for international regional experience does not suggest that such progress is achieved through concentration on trade-barrier liberalization.

As CARIFTA develops its own momentum in an orbit of interests which are of doubtful substance, greater importance attaches to the lack of operational commitment, to any additional measures of regional economic co-operation,[9] a feature which distinguishes CARIFTA from most of the regional economic schemes.

The opposing viewpoint puts the matter in terms of specific production possibilities. Although some consideration had been given in the past of the advantages of larger demand, particularly as it concerns economies of scale, little attention was paid to the possibilities of integrating the use of resources. In the latter connection, one of the outstanding and neglected features of the Caribbean is that in many ways there is a complementary range of resources—even if the present structure of output is not. This may be illustrated in the utilization of a

---

[9] The CARIFTA Council has not gone beyond authorizing the study of certain questions like the harmonization of industrial incentives a common external tariff, industrial development in the Leeward and Windward Islands.

differential land-endowment for the development of a Caribbean meat and dairy industry and in exploiting differences in sea-fertility in the development of a deep-sea-fishing industry. In the industrial field the possibilities include the use of Trinidad's oil and gas resources in the manufacture of petrochemicals leading to end-products like plastic and rubber; of Guyana's land and forest resources for textile, fibre and pulp and paper production; and of regional salt and lime resources in an industrial chemical complex involving the production of caustic soda, chlorine, etc., for regional bauxite, alumina, textile, petrochemical and paper industries.

This takes us to the political content of such an approach, the apparent lack of which has attracted a certain amount of criticism.[10] To begin with, our view is that, in current cirumstances, there is some value in testing the hypothesis that an elucidation of the economic possibilities would lead to an elucidation of the political possibilities for the reason that it was patently clear from the previous efforts that the political issues could not be formulated, let alone solved, before the economic initiatives were put forward. The argument is that one needs to know, in principle, what sort of regional economic direction governments could be induced to follow before political formulae can be advanced.

To our mind this was one of the main lessons, if not the principal one, which came out of the West Indian federal experience. If, therefore, as the Federation proved, political commitment rested upon reaction to the implications of the economic possibilities it would be premature and possibly disintegrative to devise strategies to 'harmonize' the implementation of these possibilities with vested interests, enmeshed as they are with political power. For example, a common market or economic union evidently requires a commitment of a quite different order from trade liberalization. Indeed, the production approach to regional economic integration is less far-reaching in terms of compromising national sovereignty than the approach via CARIFTA because it is selective in the extent of commitment and period of validity and because assessment of gains and losses is easily identifiable. Moreover, since it focuses on industries which do not currently exist, it avoids some of the problems which originate with vested interests.[11]

In the trade liberalization approach, for example, those who are gaining most through the freeing of trade will be least inclined to harmonize industrial incentives. Yet such a step is logically necessary

10 Aaron Segal, *The Politics of Caribbean Economic Integration*, University of Puerto Rico, 1968; Review of Studies in Regional Economic Integration, *Journal of Common Market Studies*, Vol. VII, No. 3, March 1969.
11 Cf. F. Kahnert, P. Richards, E. Stoutjesdijk, P. Thomopoulus, *Economic Integration among Developing Countries*, OECD, Paris, 1969.

if there is to be some attempt at equity in the distribution of gains. Or, having liberalized trade barriers some interests will then oppose moving to a common external tariff for the reason that it not only prejudices the conduct of an independent external commercial policy but renders it possible for the lesser developed members to use it as a bargaining mechanism for extracting concessions from the more developed members since the former will largely incur the costs of trade diversion. Yet, a common external tariff is logically the step to which free trade leads whereas in small immature economies regional import substitution is the way to national development. Indeed, in both Central America and East Africa the argument has been that the member countries, having committed themselves to over-all free trade and a common external tariff have thereby rendered it a great deal more difficult to get a production integration system working by diluting the attractiveness of such a system. So, in the case of East Africa there has been what is, in effect, a retreat to the idea that bargaining for industry may revolve on negotiations for appropriate *changes* in the common external tariff.[12] And in LAFTA the question has been whether the target for the achievement of complete free trade (recently extended from 1973 to 1980) followed by a common external tariff does not effectively diminish the drive toward the integration of the structure of production.

4. OBSTACLES AND AVENUES TO PROGRESS

The preamble to the CARIFTA treaty took note of the signatories' determination to achieve full employment and improved living standards through 'the optimum use of available human and other resources and by accelerated, co-ordinated and sustained economic development'. This raises immediately the position of Jamaica since there has been a marked absence of interest in that country in ideas going beyond trade liberalization. This has led to the view in some quarters that Jamaica ought to be excluded from CARIFTA since it will retard the pace of regional economic co-operation. On the other hand, it has appeared desirable to adopt an open policy toward Jamaica for many reasons. The Jamaican market is equal to 40 per cent of the total CARIFTA market and if this advantage can be preserved, without at the same time prejudicing future developments elsewhere in CARIFTA, then the means of so doing should be taken up. Related to this, too, is the concern that possibilities for fruitful co-operation in a wide range of other fields of considerable importance should not be closed—for example the promotion of exports and tourism, education, research, broadcasting and news reporting, currency, credits,

[12] Peter Robson, *Economic Integration in Africa*, Allen & Unwin, 1968.

international relations, professional standards, public administration, law and medicine. The desirability of promoting Jamaican participation in regional association in the ways that minimize the effect on the growth of co-operation in the rest of the Caribbean raises the question as to whether and in what ways this kind of compromise is feasible.

The background to the problem is the underdevelopment of individual Caribbean states which manifests itself in an absence of forward and backward linkages in the productive structure. It is apparent that current developments are heading for a kind of Puerto Rican situation, but without the advantage of migration outlets (to the United States) which the latter enjoys. Development through tourism possibly might be the way of curing unemployment and raising incomes, at least in some of the smaller places. But it raises a number of extra-economic issues, highlighted in societies like the Bahamas and Bermuda, which are adverse to too great a concentration upon this activity, especially for small countries whose self-image is easily destroyed. However, given the range of resources as well as the size of demand it is only by way of transnational industrial and agricultural co-operation that such linkages within the separate states of the Caribbean can evolve.

Moreover, these industrial policies are erecting in Jamaica as well as in Trinidad obstacles to progress and regional co-operation in the future. For example, the supply of materials by foreign corporations to their local associates (in industries like tyres, plastic products, steel products, paper, glass, motor vehicles and so on) imposes extremely difficult barriers to regional import substitution in these materials. Current industrialization policy in the Caribbean is therefore very much against the interest of regional development precisely in the ways which are considered to be most vital.

The Trinidadian position, whilst it has been more openly in favour of extending the commitments of CARIFTA, has not explicitly recognized this aspect of regional development. In fact, so far as policy statements go, the Trinidadian concentration seems to turn on extending the CARIFTA arrangement to other countries such as the Bahamas, Belize, the Dominican Republic, Haiti, Surinam, the Netherland Antilles and, if possible, to Martinique, Guadeloupe and Cuba. These extensions have actually been described by the Trinidadian government as the 'Next step'.[13] This takes us to the centre of the problem, the external relations of the Caribbean. Indeed, the openness of these countries renders it virtually impossible to make the usual distinctions between internal and external obstacles.

[13] Hon. Kamaluddin Mohammed, *Caribbean Integration*, Government of Trinidad and Tobago, April 1969. Mr. Mohammed is the Minister of West Indian Affairs, Trinidad & Tobago.

It might be argued in the first place that some of these possible geographical extensions of CARIFTA could provide a balancing element in the coalescence of the English-speaking Caribbean. One shortcoming, which has proved divisive elsewhere, is its concentricity— around Trinidad & Tobago and Jamaica. These two countries account for some 80 per cent of the market and population of CARIFTA. Some extension of the grouping could therefore operate to neutralize this kind of polarity. On the other hand, CARIFTA is already a complex grouping with eleven members and its extension would make it even more administratively unwieldy. More significant, however, is that the Trinidadian government's motivation may not be immediately pragmatic from an economic standpoint. Three motives may be suggested—the political prestige and historical significance of pan-Caribbeanism (a concept strongly emphasized by Prime Minister Williams in his writings); bridging the transition of a unified Caribbean bloc into the Latin American groupings; and using the possible participation of Cuba as a symbolic insulation against further indiscriminate American/European penetration possibly under the spearhead of Jamaica.

A practical assessment of the situation suggests, however, that the geographical extensions in view would render it more remote, administratively and politically, than it is now to think of economic extensions to the vital requirement of production integration. This would be particularly true should Dominica participate, given that country's current political perspectives, and it would strengthen the Jamaican outlook on regional integration. Whether the Trinidadian government would press for some relation with Cuba is a matter which has not yet come to a head, though the Trinidadian Prime Minister did call recently for a rapprochement with that country.

Given the apparently over-riding political and romantic interest of various CARIFTA members in the extension of the arrangement to other Caribbean countries, setting aside Cuba, this would probably be the least restrictive line of advance given safeguards of the kind (balance of payments, etc.) that are already incorporated in the CARIFTA treaty. The important consideration is that these extensions should not prejudice the development of initiatives in the field of production between individual states within the grouping who are so interested— for example, along the lines of the LAFTA Industrial Complementarity System, the Andean Common Market and the Regional Co-operation for Development (RCD). We shall return to this in examining internal arrangements and their potentialities for co-operation.

As regards Cuba, the approach can only be by way of an item-by-item evaluation of reciprocal trading opportunities. An attempt to apply the generalized free trade approach such as is found in the CARIFTA treaty would reduce the possible scope for compromise among differing CARIFTA members, apart from the immediately obvious fact that the notion of 'free trade' would be inoperative on the Cuban side. A common trade policy and the integration of production structures would give rise, as in the Maghreb, to virtually insoluble problems of inter-state differences in economic organization. Indeed, even within CARIFTA the move to state-trading in Guyana makes it possible to by-pass altogether the free-trade mechanism.

The differences of opinion, mainly between Jamaica on the one hand and the Eastern Caribbean on the other, on what kind of approach should be made to the EEC following Britain's prospective entry into that grouping, have recently ended with agreement to seek 'association'. This decision has resulted less as a matter of choice than from lack of feasible alternatives. The principal issue posed is the future of West Indian agricultural products—mainly sugar, bananas, citrus, cocoa, coffee and rum—which are at present protected in the United Kingdom market, should that country become a member of the EEC and have to conform to its agricultural policy.

Britain's expressed policy is to safeguard the interests of Commonwealth less-developed countries in negotiating with the Community and one aspect of this is the proposal that these countries[14] come into the EEC system under an arrangement of the Yaoundé or Arusha type. Outside of this option, countries would have to take their own chances for a commercial agreement with the EEC in specific commodities like sugar, bananas, and citrus which raise problematic question and may not be either acceptable under GATT rules or agreeable to the EEC and its associates. The decision to follow the 'association' option does not, however, remove the basic problems and on the EEC side consideration of such a status for the Caribbean is itself contingent on the outcome of a separate solution to the sugar problem.

The lack of any feasible alternative means that the approach to Europe has left controversial issues unresolved and it is therefore in order to consider some of them. First, differences in sensitivity to real or imagined breaches of national integrity and self-image are present. The European association system, indeed, has incurred in some quarters the criticism of being neo-colonialist and certainly there are aspects to the system which have given cause for doubt about the strength of its concern in practice with, for example, the promotion of the exports and development of the structure of the economies of the associated

[14] Excluding countries like India, Pakistan, Singapore, Malaysia, whose economic structure may not be judged to be similar to that of the Yaoundé associated states. Similarity in economic structure (undefined) seems to be the rationale for associate status and in the African context is so described in the Yaoundé Convention.

states.[15] Moreover, there are no indications about the durability of this system. Given the international generalization of preferences and the multilateralization of economic policies there may be even greater concern about the future significance of the association system. The progressive reduction of the EEC common external tariff (which automatically reduces the margin of preference in favour of the associated states) as well as the prospective entry into the Community of several European countries are at least indications of the possible course of future events on a broader plane. The role of reverse preferences in the maintenance of the EEC preference-area is itself a matter of some doubt, given that the EEC members other than France derive, in fact, minimal benefits from the system. Moreover, changes in French views on the subject as well as those of the African associates themselves have to be discussed in the light of alternative compensatory possibilities. This immediately brings the United States into the picture and the nature of its economic relations with Latin America as well as the, perhaps more distant, possibility of the development of African economic integration.

Secondly, there are the implications of differences in the economic structure, development and relations of the CARIFTA member countries—even if the EEC should lump them together into a homogeneous category. Jamaica's involvement with the EEC would be in a greater range of transactions than would be the case with the other members. The concessions, therefore, which would have to be granted to the EEC would be correspondingly larger so that the application of an association system to the CARIFTA grouping as a whole would involve the eastern states in disproportionate reciprocity which is equivalent to a subsidization of Jamaica's exports to Europe. At the same time, Jamaica's interest in the promotion of foreign investment is less discriminate than that of Trinidad's and Guyana's. A regional association relationship could create a propitious climate for the involvement of European private enterprise in the Caribbean. And since, moreover, CARIFTA does not provide for the allocation of new industries to individual member countries, business would tend to gravitate to Jamaica, whose market is also the largest of the member states, rather than to the eastern states. On the other hand, it is evident that the EEC does not want a multiplicity of arrangements, with a large number of very small states (including Jamaica).

Thirdly, the region's policy toward Latin America comes into focus. This involves not only an emotional element of 'third-world'

[15] The Second Yaoundé Convention gives some emphasis to the diversification of the economic structure and promotion of the exports of associated states. Convention d'Association entre la Communauté Économique et les Etats Africains et Malgaches Associés a Cette Communauté. Yaoundé, July 29, 1969 (Article 19).

identification but the longer-term economic and cultural orientation of the East Caribbean.[16] It is of note here that the latter grouping of countries has repeatedly expressed itself especially in UNCTAD against the EEC association system. From time to time, similar sentiments have been expressed with respect to the Caribbean's involvement with the Commonwealth especially in connection with schemes of economic co-operation between the latter and Latin America. We have already mentioned the interest of the Trinidadian government in Latin American economic relations and indeed in the 1967 Punta del Este Conference of Presidents of the Americas, Trinidad & Tobago gave a commitment to participate in the efforts towards the establishment of a Latin American Common Market by 1985. And in September 1968, the Prime Minister of Barbados in addressing the Organisation of American States announced his country's desire for a re-orientation of foreign economic relations toward Latin America. Guyana's failure to join the Organisation of American States and to embrace Latin Americanism more actively results from its border-conflicts with Venezuela and not from any policy away from involvement with Latin America.

On the Latin American side this interest is reciprocated, at least in principle. This may be seen, for example, in the current expressions of interest of Latin Americans and of the Economic Commission for Latin America in the convergence of sub-regional groupings in the hemisphere. The latter itself accords, though CARIFTA did not exist at the time, with the resolutions of the Presidents of the Americas that the co-ordination of groupings at the sub-regional level could facilitate the economic integration of Latin America as a whole. However, it would be premature to believe that any substantive relationship is imminent. For one thing, all the groupings in Latin America are absorbed in their own very difficult problems of integration and inter-state relations—to the point where it has led in certain countries to demands for national integration before regional integration. For another, it is still true that a wide chasm of ignorance and incomprehension divides the Commonwealth Caribbean from Latin America. Nor should it go without notice that the Latin Americans themselves have become more active recently in promoting an economic relationship with the EEC—the 'Declaration of Buenos Aires' of July 1970 calls for a 'system of co-operation'.

Associate status with the EEC raises, therefore, not only issues of political economy so far as the Caribbean states themselves are concerned, but the immediate question as to how far and in what ways it

16 It should be noted, too, that questions would also arise about the preferential relations which currently exist between Canada and the Commonwealth Caribbean should the latter become EEC associates.

compromises their initiatives toward Latin America. On both of these matters only the outlines of the main issues can be given in this paper.

So far as the internal impact is concerned, the question turns on certain obligations which associates have to undertake. Whilst associate states may levy customs duties to meet general development needs, protect infant industry and secure revenue, an association agreement such as Arusha[17] would prohibit alteration of the overall volume of concessions or the balance among individual members of the EEC. In this regard, the Yaoundé Convention is less restrictive. An association arrangement also requires the Council of Association to be informed of all tariff measures and quantitative restrictions maintained or introduced on imports from the EEC. At the request of the Council, consultations on these measures must be held and the attitude of the Community during these consultations could be (and has been, in the opinion of some African associates) a matter of importance especially when it involves protecting industries in which third countries have an interest.

With respect to the external aspect, the association system does not permit most-favoured-nation treatment to be given to third countries, whether they be Latin American or Commonwealth. Moreover, in giving positive preferences to the EEC, it introduces some discrimination against third states. These two aspects of the system seriously compromise the use of bilateral arrangements by the Caribbean as an approach to economic co-operation and integration with Latin America. Indeed, given the complex problems of Latin American groupings bilateral arrangements are probably the most feasible and possibly the only approach to economic relations with Latin America. The Trinidadian government's statement on Caribbean integration does, in fact, say that 'bilateral trade agreement should be negotiated and concluded *early* with Brazil, Venezuela, Colombia and Argentina' among other countries (including the Commonwealth ones of Australia and New Zealand). And the initiatives between LAFTA and the Central American Common Market since Punta del Este seem to envisage the Latin American 'convergence' process in a similar way, for example, through the 'industrial complementarity' system and the establishment of Latin American tariff preferences. Furthermore, whilst the association system allows, and even facilitates customs unions, free trade areas and economic co-operation agreements with third states it is a question whether those third states would view with favour their potential partners' obligations to the EEC. In the Yaoundé Convention it is, for example, provided that these relations with third states are allowable 'insofar as they are and remain compatible with the provisions of this

[17] The Agreement signed on September 26, 1969 between the EEC and the East African Economic Community comprising Kenya, Tanzania and Uganda.

Convention and, in particular, Article 11' which prohibits less favourable treatment for EEC countries than that applicable to products originating in the most-favoured third state.

This paper supports the idea that the primary political task is to extend the regional production frontier from its present restricted limits. This poses difficult problems of industry distribution and equity. Some valuable comparative experiences, both positive and negative, may, however, be drawn upon—mainly from CACM, LAFTA and RCD. We restrict ourselves here to a few conclusions with limited supporting argumentation. What all these experiences[18] seem to demonstrate is that the application only of economic principles such as location theory, comparative cost and economies of scale do not produce a sufficient measure of agreement to solve the problems of equitable distribution. Countries have differing notions about equity and place differing social values on the apparent cost of sub-optimal production in determining their national political strategies. These experiences also show that pure political negotiation as has been practised at times in East Africa, Central America and Eastern Europe can be disintegrative. The absence of an economic basis for such arrangements makes it as easy to contravene as to conclude them. It seems possible to advance the proposition that the maintenance of maximum economic sovereignty in schemes of transnational economic development should be approached not as a search for a suitable combination of economic principles but by means of procedures through which the appropriate economic rationale can be introduced into regional arrangements.

Based on these experiences certain specific lines of advance deserve attention. First, it is a more productive strategy to agree on terms to govern a transnational industrial regime than to draw up lists of regional integration-industries; and the less these terms depart from competitive conditions the greater the likelihood of coming to an agreement on location. Second, commitments should be for a fixed period of time. Political considerations reduce the ability of most countries to undertake irreversible policies. This is as true of socialist States as it is of States practising competitive party politics. Third, it is a mistake to insist that regional industrial arrangements should necessarily embrace all member countries of the grouping. The experience is that such a policy severely restricts the range of possible regional initiatives, whilst the partial approach creates conditions which are favourable to the eventual incorporation of all member countries. Fourth, it is better to locate the initiative where the interests are directly involved rather than

18 Partial treatments of the subject are found in M. S. Wionczek, 'Experience of the Central American Integration Programme as Applied to East Africa', *Industrialization and Productivity*, No. 11, 1968, United Nations; 'Industrial Integration among Developing Countries', *Asian Industrial Development News*, No. 2, 1967, United Nations.

restrict this initiative to a regional secretariat. In practice, this has been done in LAFTA and in CMEA through meetings of the industrial sectors, and in the latter also through meetings of government economic planning institutions. The problem with secretariats, apart from limited resources, is that they are inclined to over-concentration upon regionally objective arrangements evaluated on the basis of regional optimality. However, the actual experience has been that such objectivity is not specially conducive to co-operation. Greater progress seems to be forthcoming through the procedures of negotiation centred around a variety of possibilities which may be both sub-aggregate and sub-optimal.

We turn finally to offer some brief comments on the role of external pressure on regional integration in the Caribbean. The view taken here is that there is scope for this to bring a positive influence to bear on the unification of the region by contributing to the solution of some of the short-term problems raised by the movement to integration. At the moment we are seeing the development of international attitudes in favour of external stimulus being directed to the promotion of regional unity in various parts of the world. The United States after an ambivalent attitude towards Latin American regionalism swung within recent years strongly in favour of the idea to the point of pledging assistance to further these aims.[19] At the second UNCTAD the developed countries adopted a concerted declaration to the effect that they would be prepared to consider support for projects put forward with a view to surmounting some of the problems of regional integration, including assistance to the less advanced countries of regional groupings in order that they might share in the benefits of such schemes.[20] And in the current Yaoundé Convention the EEC has approved of financial aid being used to further economic co-operation in Africa, and also of loans being issued to regional development bodies.

Certain specific possibilities present themselves in the case of the Caribbean. The opportunity now exists for Britain to direct its aid policy, particularly with regard to the small islands (Leewards and Windwards), with regional objectives in mind. For example, an interesting scheme was recently put forward, in a general context, by I. M. D. Little, for the use of aid in the development of regional companies as an approach to economic integration.[21] British policy in these islands has followed the somewhat ineffectual line of meeting recurrent budget deficits, and financing social and public work projects. This,

[19] President Nixon reiterated the U.S. government's 'support of regionalism' including the 'offer of financial assistance to the Central American Common Market, the Caribbean Free Trade Area, the Andean Group and to an eventual Latin American Common Market', *United States Foreign Policy for the 1970's*, A Report by President Richard Nixon to the Congress, February 18, 1970.
[20] Decision 23(11) adopted at the New Delhi UNCTAD 1968.
[21] I. M. D. Little, 'Regional International Companies as an Approach to Economic Integration', *Journal of Common Market Studies*, Vol. 15 No. 2, December 1966.

however, has had for the most part little or no impact upon the productive structure and capability of these islands. The greater portion of the capital expenditure has not been geared directly to production, whilst the minute size of these island economies (population averaging about 80,000, and GNP about U.S. $12 million) render most productive activities, outside of agriculture, unfeasible on an island scale so far as private profit is concerned. The possibility now arising is to channel aid along the more productive lines of transnational development and also to apply it to such problems of fiscal adjustment as might be necessitated by these moves to integration. There is, as yet, no clear indication that British policy has this dimension to it.

American reaction to Caribbean integration has so far been characterized by an absence of positive initiatives in any direction, though the attitude of the United States will ultimately play a part in the way these moves develop. Many political reasons may be advanced for this apparent lack of commitment on the part of the United States. One ominous precedent, however, may be drawn from the situation as it developed in Central America. There the United States stand seemed to have favoured the free trade and even the common market idea but the integration industry regime failed to attract American sympathy and financial assistance. This was put down to American fears about monopolistic elements in the arrangement, possible state control and even discrimination against American private investors.[22] Evidently some rethinking of this position is called for since monopoly, and therefore some element of state control, are inescapable where the size of demand is small in relation to the demands of the technology employed.[23]

The latter issues are connected to the more general question of the official aid and investment policy of Britain, Canada and the United States. The recently established Regional Development Bank[24] provided an opportunity for some regionalization of these countries' economic policies by constituting it as an Integration Bank along Central American lines or even following the compromise formula of the East African Development Bank.[25] So far, this aspect has been kept to the background and the external participants have not shown themselves insistent upon the regional cohesiveness of the Bank's functions.

[22] See James D. Cochrane, 'U.S. Attitudes towards Central American Economic Integration', *Inter-American Economic Affairs*, Autumn 1964; and 'Central American Economic Integration: The "Integrated Industries" Scheme', *Inter-American Economic Affairs*, Autumn 1965.
[23] Carlos M. Castillo, *Growth and Integration in Central America*, Frederick A. Praeger, New York, 1966.
[24] Britain and Canada are contributors to the Bank's capital. The United States is not but it is ready to provide loan funds on soft terms. A question which may be asked is whether any funds so made available by the United States can, given the nature of the Bank, properly be regarded as fulfilling President Nixon's offer of financial assistance to 'support regionalism'.
[25] In practice, however, this Bank's activity to date has been exclusively concerned with national projects.

Toward an Appropriate Theoretical Framework for Agricultural Development Planning and Policy

By

GEORGE BECKFORD

In order to be effective, development planning and policy need to be informed by relevant theory. This paper at first argues that, in many important respects, the current body of agricultural development theory inadequately represents the Caribbean situation. In so far as this hypothesis is correct, it implicitly provides a partial explanation for the failure to get agriculture moving in spite of substantial government intervention and assistance in most territories of the region. It also sets the stage for the second objective of the paper: to outline some of the steps required for developing an appropriate theoretical framework and to place this selection of papers in the perspective of these considerations.

CURRENT AGRICULTURAL DEVELOPMENT THEORIES IN RELATION TO THE CARIBBEAN

Modern contributions to agricultural development theory[1] can be separated into two broad classes: those dealing with agriculture and economic development and those dealing with agricultural development *per se*. The former includes catalogues of "agriculture's contribution to overall economic development" (e.g. Nicholls, Johnston and Mellor); "growth stage theories" (e.g. Johnston and Mellor, Perkins and Witt); and "simplified mathematical models of the development process" (e.g. Fei and Ranis, Jorgenson).[2] The second category consists almost entirely of variations of one sort or another of Schultz's hypotheses about "transforming traditional agriculture".[3] The question for consideration is how well do these contributions fit the Caribbean situation?

---

[1]Two recent books which more or less provide a synthesis of these contributions to date are John Mellor, *The Economics of Agricultural Development*, Cornell University Press, 1966; and Herman Southworth and Bruce Johnston (eds.), *Agricultural Development and Economic Growth*, Cornell University Press, 1967.

[2]John W. Mellor, "Toward a Theory of Agricultural Development," (Ch. 2 of Southworth and Johnston) *ibid.*, pp. 22-23.

[3]T. W. Schultz, *Transforming Traditional Agriculture*, Yale University Press, 1964: The term "transforming traditional agriculture" now recurs consistently in all recent contributions dealing with agricultural development *per se*. So much so that one gets the uneasy feeling that North American economists regard all underdeveloped agriculture as "traditional" (in the sense described by Schultz).

SOCIAL AND ECONOMIC STUDIES, 1968, Vol. 17, No. 3, pp. 233-242.

The Nature of Caribbean Agriculture[4]

Caribbean agriculture has two main component systems of resource organization: plantation and peasant. The former is characterized by large-scale units of production with a sizeable input of hired labour, a high proportion of foreign ownership and management of resources and specialized production almost exclusively for export markets. The latter is distinguished by small-scale units of production with heavy reliance on family labour, indigenously-owned resources and mixed production patterns. Although numerically peasant units are the more important, their resource endowment and capacity for development are poor in comparison with the plantation sector.

In the West Indies, resources are very unequally distributed between the plantation and peasant sectors. Land is a critical input in agriculture; and in the island sector of the regional economy, fertile arable land is a very scarce resource. For historical reasons, the plantation sector has secured almost all the flat fertile areas and the peasant sector is poorly endowed with hillside land with shallow and relatively infertile soils. For any given combination of complementary inputs, therefore, output per acre in the plantation sector will tend to exceed that in the peasant sector. This inherent disparity in physical productivities is further exaggerated in the case of value productivities for reasons discussed below.

With the possible exception of management, the plantation sector is also better endowed with other resource inputs. By far the greater share of fixed capital in West Indian agriculture is tied up in the plantation sector. The distribution of capital is most unequal in the sugar plantation economies with roads, electricity, water supplies, machine shops, laboratories, buildings and equipment geared specifically to the production of sugar. Furthermore, the plantation sector has greater access than the peasant sector to financial capital for further capital accumulation. Imperfect competition in the capital market makes for easier credit availability and plantations can also draw on retained earnings. For labour, the peasant relies heavily on the farm family while plantation production depends on hired labour. With plentiful supplies of labour, the plantation sector has greater flexibility in adjusting labour inputs. Although the peasant sector also has access to hired labour, it can scarcely compete with the plantation sector since its relatively low land productivity weakens its competitive position.

The disparities in productivity following from the nature of resource distribution result in disparities in the returns to factors of production in a way that encourages a flow of incremental resource inputs into the plantation sector. In addition, a number of institutional factors create a dynamic bias in favour of plantation (export) output. Metropolitan preferences produce

[4]Cuba is excluded from consideration in this discussion because the organization of agriculture there is no longer the same as in the rest of the region, as was the case before 1959. Part of the discussion here draws from an earlier paper by the author. See G. L. Beckford, "Toward Rationalization of West Indian Agriculture", *Papers Presented at the Regional Conference on Devaluation*, I.S.E.R., University of the West Indies, February 2-4, 1968, mimeo.

artificially high prices and help to reduce uncertainty about future prices; technical knowledge is relatively well advanced; and marketing arrangements and infrastructure are more highly developed for plantation than for peasant production.

The foregoing considerations suggest that the plantation system of resource organization is the dominant type in the Caribbean region. The overall pattern of agricultural development is chiefly a reflection of the process of adjustment of resource use in the plantation sector. Consequently, theories of agricultural development which do not take into account the institutional characteristics of plantation-type economies can hardly be expected to fit the social reality of the Caribbean.

Agriculture and Economic Development

The literature on this topic emphasizes four main "contributions of agriculture to economic development": the supply of food and raw materials, the supply of factors to the non-agricultural sector, the earning of foreign exchange and the provision of a market for non-agricultural output.[5] The logic of the argument in such theoretical statements is based on the implicit assumption of a "closed economy" in which there are naturally strong intersectoral relationships. Since an outstanding feature of plantation economies is a high degree of "open-ness", the inter-relationships between agricultural and non-agricultural development are not very significant in such cases.

In plantation economies market inter-relationships are more important in trade with the rest of the world[6] than within the economy. Since plantation agriculture is characterized by its export orientation, the agricultural sector in such economies is geared to supplying food and raw materials to other countries and not to the non-agricultural sector. And, in turn, the plantation economy depends on other countries for its supplies of manufactures and even basic foodstuffs. This difference is important because the factors governing the terms of trade with the rest of the world do not coincide with those governing changes in the internal terms of trade.[7] There is, for example, easier mobility of labour internally than internationally.

As concerns the supply of capital for non-agricultural expansion, foreign ownership implies that this flow is depleted in plantation economies by the repatriation of dividend and interest payments. Thus the capital transfer from agriculture serves to promote non-agricultural expansion in the metropolis rather than at home. And, finally, agriculture's capacity to earn foreign exchange in plantation economies is reduced by a characteristic high import content of both production and consumption.

[5]See, for example, the chapters by Johnston and Southworth and Mellor in Southworth and Johnston (eds.), *op. cit.* and Mellor, *op. cit.*

[6]Usually the main trading partner of these countries is a metropolitan country which provides protective shelter in the form of special preferential arrangements for plantation output.

[7]Indeed, discussions in the literature suggest that in the closed models changes in the domestic terms of trade will be toward agriculture whereas the international terms of trade tend to move against plantation output.

Current development theory has so far been concerned almost exclusively with what has come to be known as "traditional agriculture". In this type of agriculture, all resources of the traditional type are said to be efficiently allocated and the rate of return to increased investment with the existing state of the arts is too low to induce further saving and investment. Consequently, development depends on breaking the established equilibrium by changes in technology involving the introduction of new "modern" inputs. The description of traditional agriculture could conceivably fit either or both sectors of Caribbean agriculture. Whether or not the description fits individual sectors, the model is of limited use in understanding the development problem because it ignores·the problem of resource allocation between sectors. As Adams recently pointed out in another connection, the traditional agriculture model does not account for the fact that efficient resource allocation on individual production units can co-exist with inefficient resource allocation for the sector as a whole.[8]

In the Caribbean, peasant operators seem to allocate resources *at their command* quite efficiently.[9] And plantation owners allocate resources efficiently *from the point of view of private accounting*. But peasant operators have insufficient resources at their command because institutional factors limit the supplies of land, capital and technical knowledge available to them. At the same time, resources tend to be under-utilized in the plantation sector. For example, available data indicate that land is seriously under-utilized in this sector. While this could represent a rational pattern of allocation and efficient resource use *for plantation owners*, it points to inefficiency for the agricultural sector as a whole. Transfer of such land to peasant operators would expand output if only because of a change in the product/factor price ratio resulting from the change in ownership — the inputs of plantation owners are likely to have a much higher opportunity cost than those of peasant operators.[10]

Particularly in the sugar plantation economies of the region, there is the further consideration that foreign ownership of resources by multi-national corporations creates certain sectoral inefficiencies and rigidities in the adjustment of resource use. The main problems involved are first that product choice is restricted and second that economic activity is of the "enclave" type. The major raw sugar producer in the region is the West Indies Sugar Co. (W.I.S.Co.), a

[8]See Dale Adams, "Resource Allocation in Traditional Agriculture: Comment" and "Reply" by Schultz in *Journal of Farm Economics*, November, 1967, as well as earlier exchanges; E. Feder, "The Latifundia Puzzle of Professor Schultz: Comment" and "Reply" by Schultz in *Journal of Farm Economics*, May, 1967; and G. L. Beckford, "Transforming Traditional Agriculture: Comment" and "Reply" by Schultz in *Journal of Farm Economics*, November, 1966.

[9]This is implicit in the findings of D. T. Edwards in his *Report on an Economic Study of Small Farming in Jamaica*, I.S.E.R., University of the West Indies, 1961.

[10]In addition to the possible expansion of output, it should be noted that the *national* income contribution per acre is likely to be higher in peasant production because there is no foreign ownership there.

wholly-owned subsidiary of Tate and Lyle which has complementary investments in shipping, sugar refining and distribution in the metropolitan markets. Adverse movements in raw sugar prices do not therefore induce changes in sugar cane production on W.I.S.Co. estates since the firm is simultaneously increasing profits on the refining end. Efficient resource use for such firms can create sectoral inefficiencies. Finally, the enclave character of the sugar plantation creates a certain artificial specificity of resource use. Thus we find plantations serviced with roads, electricity and water supplies while surrounding agricultural and rural areas are without such facilities even where there is excess capacity for plantation use.

The theoretical framework provided by the model of traditional agriculture is inappropriate for the Caribbean because structural factors create sectoral inefficiencies in resource allocation. The real danger with the traditional agriculture model is that it may provide "decision makers in developing countries . . . [with] a pseudo-sophisticated justification for overlooking possible structural changes in the agricultural sector and . . . [they] may end up placing major emphasis on politically palatable programs for bringing in new inputs from outside the sector".[11] This warning seems most appropriate for the Caribbean.

STEPS TOWARD AN APPROPRIATE FRAMEWORK

The weakness of existing theory may apply as well to other underdeveloped agriculture as to the Caribbean region. This weakness derives from a tendency to generalize from the experiences of the advanced industrialized countries and to treat underdeveloped agriculture as a more or less homogeneous class. But there are significant differences in the institutional environment as between different types of underdeveloped agriculture as well as between present day underdeveloped agriculture and that of the advanced countries at earlier periods in history. Theories which abstract from these differences must fail to reflect the realities of particular situations. What is required to begin with is a typology of world agriculture which will classify structural characteristics in some systematic way. Subsequently, theories of development relating to particular types of agriculture could be developed.[12]

Some General Considerations

Very few economists (in metropolitan countries at least) today seem to appreciate the need for the approach suggested here. One notable contribution in this direction was recently made by Phillips Foster who presented a framework for "identification of the institutional dimensions of the classical factors of production associated with any particular system of agricultural

11Dale Adams, *op. cit.*, p. 932.
12Our predecessors, the "political economists" of the more distant past saw the need for this approach and made considerable progress for particular types of agriculture. See, for example, the recently translated works of the Russian agricultural economist, Chayanov, *The Theory of Peasant Economy* (ed. Thorner, Kerblay and Smith), Irwin Inc. for the American Economic Association, 1966.

resource organization". Foster's awareness of the problem is evident from the following:

> It seems obvious that if we are going to try to transform a present-day primitive agricultural economy, we ought to know just what kind of thing we are transforming. It is *not* the same primitive agriculture which has already been transformed in the process of producing the highly industrialized western democracies. The cultural milieu which produced "the West" included strong elements of Puritan protestantism, a north-European land tenure system, a philosophy that hard work is good *per se*, a respect for the scientific method of investigation, etc. The non-Western world today is certainly not a carbon copy of the Western world in A.D. 1500, nor of the Western world in any other period of its history. Unfortunately, we don't really know much about the structure of the agricultural systems which we are trying to transform now in the late twentieth century.[13]

Foster's framework will provide useful insights at the micro level. But it requires parallel research on macro problems that derive from particular socio-economic and political situations.

At a very rudimentary level, we can identify five major types of agriculture which have existed in various parts of the world and which reflect different socio-economic and political situations: (1) the "feudal" system which existed in Europe before the Industrial Revolution and which still exists in certain areas of the world; (2) the "commercial family-farm" system which characterized the settler-homestead agricultural economies of North America, Australia, New Zealand and Europe after the Industrial Revolution and which is still the dominant system in these countries; (3) the "plantation" system which, with colonization, came to dominate the economies of the Caribbean, much of Central and South America, southern United States and South-east Asia; (4) the "peasant" system of which there are two sub-types: one relating to subsistence production and the other to market-oriented production, as in parts of Africa (exports) and Japan (for the domestic market); and (5) the "state-controlled" systems of contemporary China and Eastern Europe.

Historical evidence indicates that the rate of agricultural progress and overall economic growth has, on the whole, been considerably higher in Western Europe, North America, Australia, New Zealand and Japan than in other regions of the world.[14] And it is perhaps of some significance that the agricultural sectors of these countries are, with one exception, dominated by the commercial family-farm system. The exception is Japan which was placed in the category of peasant production for the domestic market. These two categories are in fact quite similar to each other — the only major structural difference being in respect of the size of units of production.

The commercial family-farm system has a number of features which are

13Phillips Foster, "Analyzing Systems of Agricultural Resource Organization", *Journal of Farm Economics*, May 1966, p. 272.

14It is perhaps too early to judge the relative performance of those economies which are dominated by export-based peasant systems and state-controlled systems. Both systems are of relatively recent vintage.

conducive to sustained development.[15] First, it involves a more equitable distribution of land and of income than any of the other systems. As a result, the effective demand for the output of other domestic industries is relatively great and this provides inducement for the development of non-agricultural activities. In addition, savings and investment are widely dispersed throughout the economy. Second, the heavy reliance on family labour limits the supply of available labour and thereby induces technological change of a kind in which modern inputs are continuously substituted for labour. Third, the infrastructure (including economic institutions) tends to be well developed *spatially* and therefore encourages widespread development of other activities. Fourth, the social and political environment is geared to the well-being of the *whole* population.

None of the other systems listed above has this combination of characteristics. In general, the relatively retarded nature of those systems can be *partly* related to (a) the "open-ness" of the system (plantation and export-based peasant) which weakens intersectoral links within those economies and/or (b) gross inequalities in the distribution of wealth and income (feudal and plantation) which keeps effective demand at a low level and restricts savings and domestic investment. These are only superficial and partial explanations. There are many other economic factors which need to be considered. In addition the social, cultural, political and other non-economic elements that influence human behaviour must be integrated into the analysis of development performance. The intention here is simply to provide a brief insight in order to justify the analytical approach being suggested. So far most of the research effort on the development process has been directed to the commercial family farm system and the peasant system. But even in these cases our understanding of the processes at work is limited because of the failure to forge inter-disciplinary studies of the problems. On account of this heritage, it is now impossible to analyse in any depth how institutional factors influence the pattern of development of different types of agriculture.

The Development Problem in Plantation Economies

In any typology of world agriculture, the plantation system of resource organization would have a distinct place. Its combination of metropolitan export orientation, foreign ownership and the particular technological nature of the production function create conditions which *determine* a particular pattern of development.[16] Furthermore, the social stratification, class differences and distribution of political power which characterize plantation societies influence the development process in particular ways.[17]

[15]For further discussion of some of these considerations, see Robert Baldwin, "Patterns of Development in Newly Settled Regions", *The Manchester School of Economic and Social Studies*, May 1956.

[16]Baldwin, *op. cit.*, has demonstrated that the nature of the production function *alone* is decisive.

[17]For elaboration on this point see, for example, R. T. Smith, "Social Stratification, Cultural Pluralism and Integration in West Indian Societies" in S. Lewis and T. G. Mathews, *Caribbean Integration*, Rio Piedras, Puerto Rico, 1967.

111

Some important characteristics of plantation agricultural economies are as follows:

(i) production is based on large-scale units utilizing a sizeable resident labour force performing routine tasks for close to subsistence wages;

(ii) production is oriented to metropolitan export markets in which protective shelter is provided;

(iii) foreign capital, entrepreneurship and management govern economic activity;

(iv) export production consists of a narrow range of primary commodities; and

(v) a small planter class (and/or their metropolitan connections) have great political power and high social status involving a certain social antipathy towards the bulk of the population.

A number of economic consequences flow directly from these characteristics. First, resource availability is not simply determined by the factor endowments of the particular country because the system itself is defined as being dependent on factors of production which, with the exception of land, are all drawn from abroad. Second, resource use is determined by the economic interests of the foreign owners. Where these are multi-national corporations with complementary investments in processing and marketing the plantation output, resources are directed to the specific needs of the corporation for raw material inputs.[18] And this creates a built-in rigidity in the pattern of resource adjustment. Third, the level of aggregate effective demand will always tend to be low since the bulk of the population have low incomes which are not allowed to rise significantly. Fourth, the plantation system is likely to generate chronic underemployment over time because of fluctuations in export prices and the fixed nature of the labour supply. Fifth, foreign ownership implies that much of the saving and investment potential is depleted by the outflow of factor payments in the form of interest and dividends; while retained foreign earnings "tend to be employed for further expansion of the export industry, since foreign investors prefer investments which are directly linked with the foreign exchange earning ability of the economy".[19] Sixth, the external orientation of economic activity dampens internal intersectoral relationships; and investment does not provide any significant multiplier effects. Seventh, the termination of production at the primary stage prevents the development of significant forward and backward linkages and this results in weak spread effects from agricultural development.

Over time, the prospects for development both within and outside of agriculture are limited for a number of reasons. To begin with, the small size of the market — a consequence of the low level of effective demand — limits the development of large-scale industries. Market demand for non-export

---

[18]Tate and Lyle sugar operations in the West Indies and United Fruit Company banana operations in Central America are outstanding examples of this situation.

[19]Robert E. Baldwin, op. cit.

agricultural production is therefore low; the small high-income land-owning class satisfy their requirements with imports. On the supply side also, there are several factors which impede agricultural progress. Technological change is slow because additional resource inputs are continuously secured from abroad. When land (the only resource input supplied by the economy) becomes scarce in a particular country, the multi-national corporation solves the scarcity problem by expanding production in some new country. Periods of adverse export prices may induce technological change only if this places an excessive burden on profits.

Diversification of farm output is restricted partly because of the specific raw material needs of the plantation corporation and partly because the structure of output prices favours the sheltered export crop. In addition, very little technical knowledge concerning production of other crops is acquired because agricultural research is export biased. Marketing and credit are geared mainly to export crops and where land is scarce resident farmers have relatively little access to fertile land and other resources. Because of low incomes, they do not have the wherewithal to acquire additional resources; and the ruling class use their political power to maintain the *status quo*.

Scraps of evidence lend some support to the foregoing propositions. Furtado's celebrated study of the economic growth of Brazil provides much insight into the processes which have accounted for stagnation in the plantation economy of the North-east.[20] The relatively poor performance of the U.S. South can no doubt be also explained in similar terms.[21] And the economic histories of the Caribbean, Central and parts of South America seem to follow closely the pattern described by Furtado. For South-east Asia, Myrdal has recently provided us with partial explanations for what he describes as the "weak spread effects from the development spurts in (plantation) agriculture".[22] But so far we have only fleeting glimpses of the problem and there is as yet no systematic formulation of ideas which could provide even a sketch of an appropriate theory.

The present collection of papers is intended to help fill the existing gap. The collection is largely Caribbean in orientation, historical in scope, empirical in method, and to some extent inter-disciplinary in approach. Such a combination is warranted for the purpose at hand. The general picture that emerges substantiates the view that there are numerous elements in the social

[20]His analysis of the mechanism of the slave plantation economy during the 16th and 17th centuries is particularly illuminating. The analysis concludes as follows: "the sugar economy . . . managed to resist the most protracted of depressions for more than three centuries, achieving some degree of recuperation whenever conditions in the external market permitted, without being compelled to undergo any significant structural changes." See Celso Furtado, *The Economic Growth of Brazil*, Berkeley and Los Angeles, pp. 43-58.

[21]See Douglass North, *The Economic Growth of the United States: 1790-1860*, Prentice Hall, Englewood Cliffs, N.J., 1961.

[22]Gunnar Myrdal, *Asian Drama: An Inquiry into the Poverty of Nations*, Pantheon, New York, 1968, pp. 447-452. This monumental three-volume work provides a great deal of insight into the more general problem of the relevance of existing social science theory for underdeveloped countries.

and institutional structure of plantation-type economies which impede general economic development. The "case study" of development performance in Barbados suggests that conventional policies tend to induce little or no change in economies of this type.

The concluding hypothesis, then, is that underdevelopment in the Caribbean emanates directly from the particular social and institutional character of the plantation system of resource organization. And the problem of development is one that must involve changes in that structure.

RESOLVING THE THREE-HORNED PLANNING DILEMMA

Albert Waterston

Three major approaches are discernible in the literature concerned with the theory and practice of planning. The first is the conventional form generally accepted today which seeks to maximize benefits through rational choice of means from among available alternatives to achieve specific objectives; the emphasis is on these objectives. Conventional planning is usually embodied in a global, multiannual plan. The second approach takes as its point of departure available resources, and seeks to optimize benefits from these. It usually relies on sophisticated econometric techniques. The third approach is a partial, frequently intuitive, approach to planning which attempts to achieve results on a piecemeal basis. None of these approaches, in my view, offers a viable resolution of the planning dilemma; I believe that a new conceptual framework is required to meet current needs.

Each of the three major planning approaches has its adherents. The first approach—*conventional planning* —probably has a majority among planning advocates; the second—*planning by optimization*—has fewer advocates, but the number is growing as more technicians with the required skills graduate from universities and enter the field; the third—*partial planning*—has the fewest advocates, although, as anyone who has observed planning in practice can testify, it has many more practitioners than the other two approaches combined. There are good reasons for this.

It is not that partial planning is necessarily better than conventional planning. In theory, it is always worse; it is only in practice that it frequently proves to be better. That is why it persists. In theory, conven-

FINANCE AND DEVELOPMENT, 1972, Vol. 9, No. 2, pp. 36-41.

tional planning provides perspective, comprehensiveness, and internal consistency. These virtues cannot be claimed for partial planning. Yet, when put to the test, conventional planning has often had less success than partial planning.

Conventional planning is frequently criticized, but it goes too far to say, as sometimes happens, that it has failed. Still, it must be admitted that the results obtained from it, at the urban as well as at the regional or national level, are not impressive. Partly, this is because of methodological shortcomings; partly, it is because of the inhospitable environment in which conventional planning often operates; but mostly, it is because conventional planning does not meet social needs. It is in the last connection, perhaps, that it is most nearly right to say that conventional planning has failed; for it is here that the gap between aspiration and achievement often yawns wide. It would be a mistake to interpret this as a case of practice giving the lie to theory, since practice without theory is an absurdity; it is rather a demonstration of persistence in the application of wrong theory.

THE IMPLICATIONS OF CONVENTIONAL PLANNING

The framework of conventional planning is very familiar. On the basis of objectives set by the political leadership, and with planned targets fixed or approved by it, planners (who are usually cast in the role of neutral technicians outside the political arena) derive optimal resource allocations and then select, from feasible alternatives, policies and instruments for achieving planned targets. Implementation of the plan is the responsibility of technical departments and agencies concerned with the different sectors or programs covered by the plan; supervision and control over plan implementation are usually the responsibility of the political authority.

This logically structured approach is defensible if each step in the procedure is rational in itself and is rationally related to the other steps. Specifically, the procedure outlined is justifiable if, first, the conceptual framework or model on which the plan is based is internally consistent; second, if the variables of the model incorporated in the plan are the crucial ones for the social unit concerned; third, if the data on which the plan is based are reasonably accurate and complete; fourth, if the implicit assumptions in the plan concerning the environment in which the plan is to be implemented are correct; and, fifth, if the plan's objectives adequately reflect social needs. Examination of these elements exposes serious flaws in the conventional approach to planning.

Internal Consistency

Consider the matter of internal consistency. Because much of what passes for planning is ad hoc and based on hunch, planning specialists understandably put a heavy premium on internal consistency. There is much to be said in favor of the rationality inherent in an internally consistent, integrated plan. Not only does it relate inputs to outputs; it also reveals the interrelationships of factors affecting development. But, it is very difficult to formulate an internally consistent plan. Not surprisingly, therefore, most plans fail on this score.

The Missing Variables

However, even when a reasonable level of internal consistency is achieved, the results are frequently of little practical value because they give only partial answers to planning problems. Because analytical complexity increases with the number of variables used, planners include as few variables as possible, an approach that necessarily constricts the limits of possible answers. By posing questions shielded from outside disturbance or uncertainty, answers are bound to be simplistic; by narrowing the scope of problems, solutions are sure to be circumscribed.

Because they usually stake out and lay claim to a very limited field, planners make it intellectually manageable to deal with; but because they exclude so many variables which enter into actual decision making, they diminish the relevance and usefulness of the results they have obtained. Thus, one might say that while they are somewhere in the stadium, it is not where the game is being played. Planners' preference for internal consistency over practicality or feasibility also helps explain why, at the national level in most countries, economic planning goes forward without anything like adequate attention to social, political, spatial, and ecological aspects of the choices being made.

The Data Gap

Conventional planning is also especially vulnerable to data inadequacies which, it must now be recognized, are not going to be overcome soon. All planning requires data, but aggregative, integrated planning of the conventional variety is an insatiable consumer of statistical and other information. Every planner knows that there are always gaps in the data he uses and that available statistics are frequently unreliable. Not only are parameters often little more than guesses, but basic data for population, population growth and migration, households, businesses, production, income, and standards of living, as well as many of the components of national and regional income accounts, are at best suspect and often nonexistent.

The data gap makes it difficult to plan partially or globally; but the danger of compounding errors is greater when inaccurate data are incorporated in a plan which by its nature is required to be internally consistent. What is being made internally consistent in most plans are bad statistics, not realities. Whereas a careful planner is aware of the limitations of his data, and qualifies his conclusions accordingly, most political leaders do not comprehend the low reliability of the data with which planners must work. Usually, therefore, political leaders accept without understanding the figures in the plans they adopt, thereafter giving official sanction to error and incompleteness.

Mistaken Assumptions About the Environment

Deficiencies in internal consistency, in the definition of the planning problem, and in the data used, provide clues about why conventional plans have performed below expectation and need. Even more important clues are furnished by an examination of the assumptions implicit in conventional plans about the environment in which these plans must be implemented. Since such plans say little or nothing about how and who is to start the whole process going by hurdling the political, economic, and administrative obstacles which usually prevent giving effect to the plans' prescriptions, they cannot be said to be rationally related to the environment which they are presumably designed to change.

The crisis in planning is most apparent when the

118

time comes to implement plans. This does not mean, as many think, that there is a crisis of implementation. On the contrary, it is much more a crisis of plan formulation because relevant means of implementation are not adequately provided for when the plans are being formulated.

When, as in conventional planning, the planning process begins with objectives and targets, and proceeds "from the top down" as it were, to the choice of strategies, policies, instruments, measures, and projects to achieve the targets and objectives of a plan, two assumptions are implicit in the procedure: the first is that once objectives and targets have been fixed, planning can provide a technical or scientific way of realizing them; and the second is that the environment can and should be changed to give effect to the technical solutions proposed.

The Separation of Ends and Means

It is very doubtful whether the imponderables and unstructured complexities which surround most planning problems can be satisfactorily handled by any model (or plan) that takes its rationale from the consistency of numerical relationships. As noted, too many of the variables cannot be satisfactorily measured or weighted. Given objectives, constraints, and time horizon, it is possible for planners to provide technical planning solutions in the limited sense that they can maximize, on paper, outputs for given inputs. But even here, there is the difficulty that precisely defined objectives are hard to come by. Frequently, objectives are vague, ambiguous, or in conflict with one another; and when objectives are uncertain, neat technical solutions are impossible.

What is more important, although solutions may be *produced* by technical means, they cannot be *applied* as technical solutions to a planning problem. Each solution exacts its price and involves certain consequences. The application of one solution may be acceptable politically and socially, while another may not. Hence, it is naïve to assume that the setting of objectives and targets is a political act and the formulation of strategies, policies and measures for achieving objectives and targets is a technical act. Planning ends and means should be inseparable. More than any other reason, the separation of the formulation of plans from the provision of the means for their implementation accounts for the wide gulf between what is planned and what is achieved.

The second assumption implicit in the conventional planning process—that the environment must be reoriented to give effect to the solution prescribed for achieving plan objectives and targets—really rests on the first assumption. For if it is true that the method of implementing a plan has been technically, i.e., scientifically, determined, it is proper that the civil service and the public administration be altered as needed to carry out the planners' prescription.

But this is easier said than done. Experience shows that major adjustments in the organization of the public administration or in the way civil servants conduct their business take a great deal of effort and time— usually the time of several plans. Thus, any plan whose implementation depends on major reorganization of the public administration or big changes in the way civil servants do things is in trouble before it begins.

Objectives and Needs

Despite what has been said, even the most confirmed critic must admit that conventional plans have often yielded results which could not have been produced without these plans. Indeed, it is partly because of these successes that traditional planners are still in great demand. By pointing to the successes, planners have an easy answer for those who question whether conventional planning achieves its objectives.

But the problem of planning objectives is not answered by occasional success in fulfilling plan targets. For it is becoming increasingly apparent that planning "successes," even when they conform to plan objectives and targets, too often fail to meet essential needs. Thus, nations with good records for achieving their growth targets have nevertheless made little headway in dealing with basic problems like unemployment, greatly skewed income distribution, malnutrition, inadequate housing, urban and rural slums, and abject poverty of substantial parts of their populations—all of which national development is supposed to ameliorate if not eliminate.

One conclusion seems inescapable: the objectives found in traditional plans are often inappropriate for solving basic social problems. It is not a question of

120

getting political authorities to change the objectives. The real question is whether it is possible for anyone in the center of government at any level to be adequately informed about the precise objectives required to meet the basic needs of different constituencies. Scattered evidence indicates that it may be possible in backward societies, but not in others. In the U.S.S.R. central planning has achieved considerable successes where local needs could be postponed or ignored, but attempts by central planners to predict, or respond to what they thought were local needs have faltered badly. Yugoslavia, with perhaps the greatest experience with planning at different political levels, concluded as long ago as the early 1950s that planners in Belgrade could not inform themselves sufficiently to be able to fix planning ends and means consonant with the differing social needs of the various republics, districts, and communes in the country. The growing regional consciousness visible in many countries also makes it clear that planning objectives and means for achieving them determined in a national capital cannot hope to meet social needs as they are seen and felt within each region.

OPTIMIZATION PLANNING

It is essentially for these reasons that refinements and improvements primarily directed toward overcoming technical inadequacies in plan formulation are unlikely to succeed where traditional planning has failed. And optimization planning is only a refinement of traditional planning. For while traditional planners are content to allocate resources "efficiently" (economists' jargon for getting the most growth out of the available resources), planners who seek "optimal" results try to allocate resources centrally to obtain the greatest possible satisfaction of wants. The goal of conventional planning is general economic growth; the goal of optimization planning is the satisfaction of a bundle of specific wants.

But there are excellent reasons for doubting the existence of any ideal bundle of society's collective wants. Nor is it likely that the solution to this problem will be found, as some contend, in future research for improved techniques and planning models designed to permit the use of imperfect data. The difficulty is that it is improbable that logically structured solutions are possible in a situation in which planning problems are almost invariably surrounded by a host of indeterminate and imponderable elements.

This difficulty cannot be overcome by the use of mathematical methods. Mathematics is a form of shorthand logic: it may facilitate logical analysis through the transposition into mathematical symbols of verbal descriptions of what may happen under certain circumstances. But this transposition does not constitute an advance toward proving anything. The use of mathematics in this way merely restates verbal arguments in mathematical terms—no more.

Econometrics goes further, since it involves the application of mathematical and statistical procedures to the explanation, prediction, and control of economic phenomena. Great advances have been made in the use of econometric techniques in the last few decades and the outlook is for further advances. Econometrics can, and will undoubtedly continue to, throw useful light on the interrelationships between variables which enter into the planning process. However, what has been said about the limitations of any approach which seeks to provide formal solutions to problems which are essentially unstructured, prevents one from feeling unduly optimistic about the potentialities of econometrics as a means of solving important planning problems.

PARTIAL PLANNING

We arrive, finally, at partial planning. Partial planning actually includes several variants. At the national level, these may include programs for the public part of an economy; programs for a single economic or social sector; so-called "bottleneck" planning, in which projects are begun only when an acute shortage of an important commodity is imminent or already exists; or where individual projects are selected on an ad hoc basis without any overall framework. Planning of this kind has very obvious defects, and has been described in such terms as "balloon shooting" and "project snatching." However, it is often resorted to and its continuance shows that it meets some need. That is perhaps all that can be said in its favor.

RESOLVING THE PLANNING DILEMMA

The question therefore arises whether there is another

approach which is better equipped than conventional, optimization, or partial planning to deal effectively with the social problems that these do not seem to be able to resolve. It is clear that such an approach has to have a built-in mechanism for identifying and solving these problems. Lack of such a mechanism makes it difficult to connect objectives and targets in conventional plans to basic social problems in need of solution.

Generally, objectives in conventional plans aim to achieve the solution of such problems indirectly. For example, by setting as an objective a rate of growth for the gross national product which exceeds the rate at which the population is growing, national planners hope that higher per capita incomes will be widely realized and not be merely an average that could hide increasing inequalities. At the urban level, planners hope gradually to reduce urban blight by the implementation of a design incorporated in a master plan. But as experience has now demonstrated, these developments fail to materialize so many times that the failures cannot be dismissed as exceptions in a pattern of success.

When the planning process begins with the setting of objectives that are only indirectly aimed at specific social problems, it is uncertain whether the realization of the objectives will in fact meliorate these problems. Any indirect means of resolving problems runs this risk. But there is no sense in trying to solve critical social and economic problems indirectly solely because traditional planning tools of analysis require it. This way of solving problems makes needs serve planning, when planning should serve needs. Furthermore, a direct approach is available. A *problem-oriented* approach has been tried and has been found to be responsive to the solution of social problems.

If the planning process begins with a rigorous evaluation of all the pertinent information about the environment, without regard for disciplinary boundaries, in the course of which specific problems requiring solution are identified, it becomes possible to select means appropriate to the resolution of the problems. The process by which these means are determined requires an evaluation of the real and financial resources, and the identification of the economic, social, political, institutional, administrative, physical, ecological, informational, and other constraints. Because the means selected to solve the planning problems are keyed to the

STEPS IN THE PLANNING PROCESS

Conventional Planning Approach

1. Setting objectives

2. Setting targets (quantified objectives)

3. Devising a strategy for achieving targets

4. Selecting policies and projects

5. Reconciling resources with requirements

6. Solving essential social problems

Problem-Oriented Approach

1. Identifying the essential social problems to be resolved

2. Reconciling these with available resources

3. Selecting projects and policies to help solve the problems

4. Devising a strategy for resolving the problems

5. Setting targets (and time horizons)

6. Choosing overall objectives based on the social problems to be resolved

environment in which implementation will occur, they do not suffer from the incompatibility between means and environment encountered in conventional plans. After the means for dealing with the problems are selected, it becomes feasible to set realistic targets and objectives within a fixed time horizon.

Thus, as the table indicates, the problem-oriented approach follows a sequence which turns out to be the reverse of the conventional one. A problem-oriented approach to planning, starting, as it were, from the bottom up, ends the plan formulation process with *highly specific* objectives derived from the problems to be solved (e.g., at the national level, it might be the raising of per capita incomes of those below the national average to the average). This is in considerable contrast to the objectives in traditional plans, which are usually too *highly aggregated* to meet the varying needs of different constituencies (e.g., at the national level, increasing the national income by a fixed percentage annually). Such overaggregation is almost inevitable in plans made at the center of government since planners there cannot possibly be well enough informed to identify the varying high-priority problems in different localities, as well as the resources available for dealing with these problems.

Moreover, a problem-finding and problem-solving approach to plan formulation is more promising than other planning approaches because it is purposively multidisciplinary in orientation, thereby making it easier to deal more effectively than a unidisciplinary approach with the social, economic, political, institutional, physical, and ecological facets of problems. While the intrinsically amorphous nature of many planning problems makes the proposed approach more heuristic and unstructured than traditional planning, there is no reason why projects chosen for execution in the various constituencies cannot and should not be integrated into programs for economic and social sectors. These can then be integrated into comprehensive short-term and long-term plans for an entire economy, a region, or an urban or rural area. The suggested approach also provides manifold opportunities for the use of sophisticated planning techniques, including cost-benefit calculations, systems analysis, and program and performance budgeting in the direct identification and solution of high-priority social problems.

In contrast with the use of these techniques to help achieve the characteristically global objectives of planning from the top down, the use of these techniques in conjunction with planning from the bottom up increases their relevance for resolving specific social problems. Because of this, and because of its multidisciplinary nature, the suggested approach can be more truly comprehensive than the traditional approach.

The Need for Decentralization

Planning on the basis of a problem-identification and problem-solving approach requires that the planning process be decentralized. While broad strategies and policies must be centrally determined, the widest authority must be delegated to local communities and bodies to plan for themselves. In Yugoslavia, where success in planning depends greatly on an incentive system which requires the participation of virtually everyone engaged in economic and social activities, it has been established after much experimentation that the commune, the smallest territorial unit in the political structure—and within the commune, the firm—is usually the best judge of its problems and priority needs.

Attempts to delegate planning authority to local communities have often produced unsatisfactory results. But this has almost always been due to a lack of technical skills or resources, or both. Resources by themselves are not sufficient. Without technical assistance to help put resources to productive use (where the skill to do so is not available indigenously), resources are frequently squandered. Where the delegation of authority has been accompanied with enough resources to get a program started and with the appropriate kind of technical assistance to show the local people how to organize themselves to do better what they want to do (and not, as often happens, how to do what the outside technicians think the local people ought to be doing), the results have been good.

Coordination

There is, of course, the problem of coordination, and not only at one level. It is essential to see national, regional, urban, rural, and local planned development as aspects of the same thing, just as countries are beginning to see national development and planning as aspects of international regional development and planning. Coordination is an important task of all planning units. But it should be exercised in a way which encourages maximum participation of those who are affected by the plan. It should be obvious that a planning system which seeks to improve the lot of people can profit from built-in methods for eliciting the fullest possible participation of those concerned. This implies that planners must work closely with existing communal organizations where they exist and to help establish them where they do not.

This article is a condensed and modified version of the O'Harrow Memorial Lecture which the author presented at the 1971 Meeting of the American Society of Planning Officials. The original lecture appears in Planning 1971 *published by the Society.*

COLONIALISM, NATIONALISM, FRACTIONALISM
AND SELF-IDENTITY AMONG GUYANESE LEADERS

Ralph C. Gomes

Becoming an independent nation and shedding
the shackles of colonialism do not happen
simultaneously for the Guyanese people. Despite the popular slogan "Backra day done"
meaning the white man's day is over, the
present conditions in Guyana tend to question this assertion. The colonial structure
of the society continues to persist with all
of its ramifications. The heritage of
racial tensions engineered by the colonialists, foreign-owned industries, together
with the mushrooming of factionalism, make
the outlook for Guyana's Cooperative
Republic very troubled indeed. This
paper traces the actions of the leaders;
their problems, and the dilemmas they face.

Guyana, a former colony of Britain with an approxi-
mate area of 83,000 square miles and an estimated
population of 687,000, is situated on the northern coast
of South America. Guyana became an independent nation
on May 26, 1966 and a Cooperative Republic on February
23, 1970. The ethnic composition in 1964 was: Indo-
Guyanese 50.16 percent; Afto-Guyanese and Mixed Colored
43.2 percent; Amerindian 4.6 percent; Portuguese 1.0 percent;
Chinese 0.6 percent and British 0.4 percent.

World War II was the beginning of the end of European
political domination of under-developed regions. The
decade following saw bursts of nationalist movements under
the direction of western education elites demanding and
receiving what was their right-full participation in and
control over their own destinies.

The process of the transformation from colony to nation
brings about changes in the norms, structural arrangements,
practices of groups, and also have differential impact
within the social system. For example, some groups will
feel it to be detrimental to their material or ideal

ORIGINAL MANUSCRIPT.

interest, while others will feel their positions strengthened through its introduction. Change, no matter what its source, breeds strain, conflicts and cleavages.

THE COLONIALIST FRAMEWORK OF CONTROL
The Motivational Base of the Nationalist Movement

It is clear to the student of nationalism that colonialism weaves a web of discontent out of which nationalist movements have arisen. It is equally clear that a colonial society, involves among other things, a de-facto power position of the colonialists, segregation in various degrees between the over-lords and the natives, and various policies based on the supremacy premise.

In the pre-World War II period of colonialization of Guyana, and until fairly recently, Guyana was under the domination of an alien group - Colonialists-claiming various rights and privileges. Both Smith (1962) and Newman (1964) raised the questions of how a small minority of Europeans successfully controlled the much larger population. They concluded that this was not done so much by strict discipline and employment of a trained militia, but rather by setting up a rigid hierarchial social structure bounded by two extremes. At the apex of the structure, the colonialists reigned supreme with an air of superiority and made up in status and power what they lacked in numbers. At the base of the social scale were the masses who were looked down upon and whose condition was, in general, pitiful. This European-dominated structure affected the Guyanese people. For, out of this relationship of "superior-inferior" the essential social structure of the society was organized with a value system based on color and "Englishness". In other words, a value system graded from white to black. English culture became the basis on which everything was judged. Smith (1962) sums up the situation by declaring that:

The Negroes, the Colored, and the English-
speaking whites all came to share a common
conception of the colonial society; a conception in which things English and "white"
were valued highly whilst things African
and "black" were valued lowly (p.41).

This value scale based on "Englishness" led many
Guyanese to assimilate the colonialist culture.
Schools and churches established by the colonialists
were aimed at making Guyanese English in cultural outlook i.e. English in values, attitudes and morals,
while alienating them from their natural source of
cultural identity. In essence, the policies and actions
of the Colonialists encouraged Guyanese to deprecate
the worthiness of their folk culture, and thus weaken
their traditional social relationships. As Smith
(1962) observed:

> The devaluation of folk culture and the
> growing emphasis on the value of anything
> "English" in origin...had its evils, the
> greatest of them being the separation of
> the bulk of the population from the source
> of its values. In school, children learned
> about the English country-side, English
> history, and they read English literature.
> In itself this was no bad thing; the diffi-
> culty was that they could not identify
> themselves as "English" and were not encouraged
> to think of themselves or their immediate
> surroundings as interesting, valuable, or
> potentially creative (pp. 203-204).

In 1966, Prime Minister Forbes Burnham, had occasion
to comment that:

> Like so many other people achieving indepen-
> dence in our generation we have had our lives
> and our habits influenced and shaped by cen-
> turies of colonial rule...causing us to
> ignore and sometimes consciously condemn our

own acheivements and distinctive cultural
patterns.

In the same statement he continued:

> We have been satisfied to accept the European
> description of our forefathers' revolutions
> and struggles as mere riots and rebellions
> against lawful authority, instead of part
> of pattern of a subject people's struggle
> to recapture their freedom (Burnham 1966, p.2).

Administratively, the policies and actions of the
colonialists made control of Guyanese easier. Psychologically, such control, created an erosion of
reference group ties, loss of stable ego-anchorages
and had implications of loss of cultural identity and
self-respect for Guyanese. Despite the natives'
acquisition of the white man's values, opinion and
style of life, they were nevertheless regarded as
fundamentally different and inferior. Several
rituals of avoidance were practised to reinforce the
distinctions. For example:

> It was the 'done' thing to invite Colored
> people of certain class level to sugar estate
> staff dances or parties, but rarely to private
> parties or informal gatherings in the home;
> it was permissible for young British bachelors
> to have casual affairs with local girls but
> they were not expected to marry them; it was
> permissible to mix with local Colored elites
> at public functions but not to belong to the
> same club or lodge (Smith 1962, p. 85).

The fundamental problem was not the racial snobbery
proper, but rather its implications of damaged self -
image and identity of Guyanese. Or as Smith (1962)
puts it!

> The really important thing, however, was that
> the Negroes themselves accepted their inferiority.

The term 'nigger' was used in a prejorative sense amongst themselves; to be a creole was accounted better than being African-born; to be a double creole' even better (p. 41).

The inherent threat to Guyanese identity and integrity, along with social injustice, invariably produced various sporadic reactions. In their manifest forms they ranged from slave revolts to labor union protests, and later-after World War II - into a comprehensive national movement. The early phases of revolts and protests were more of a mood than an organized force. Nevertheless, the Berbice slave rebellion in 1763 was one of the first semi-successful attempts denouncing the established power structure. The rebellion struck the first blow for Guyanese independence (King 1966, p.22)

Again in 1808, 1823, and 1826, slave revolts broke out. These revolts sought among other things to redress the wrongs to Guyanese. The leaders of the revolts appealed for the very thing they had been taught to expect from the British overlords - ie. self-respect and integrity, freedom and equality and better living and working conditions.

From 1915 to the early 1940's prior to the emergence of nationalist political parties, a variety of reactive movements emerged. Two national ethnic associations were founded. The first of these was the East Indian Association founded by Joseph Ruhoman, an East Indian journalist. It became fully established under the aegis of J.A. Luckhoo, a British trained lawyer also of East Indian descent. Almost parallel was the League of Colored Peoples founded by Dr. C.H. Denbow, an American trained dentist of African descent. Both of these associations spoke on behalf of the political, social and cultural needs associated with their respective ethnicity. Two labor unions were also organized along racial lines. The British Guiana Labor Union was founded by a black nationalist, H.M. Critchlow representing Black dock workers; while the Man-Power Citizens Association was organized by Ayube

Edun, a British educated East Indian, representing East
Indian Workers on the sugar estates.

Using their middle class perspectives, these leaders
through their associations and unions raised moderate
demands for change. They were mostly concerned with
the abuses of the colonial policy and paid very little
attention to the very idea of colonialism. However,
these associations and labor unions after World War 11
were used as spring boards for political office by
politicians such as L.F.S. Burnham, John Carter, Dr.
Lachmansingh, Jai Narine Singh, Cheddi Jagan and others.
The associations and Unions actually gave birth to the
nationalist political party and were instrumental in the
people's drive towards self-determination.

THE SIGNIFICANCE OF ALIENATION AND SOCIO-CULTURAL DISORGANIZATION AS A BASIC VARIABLE IN THE RISE AND GROWTH OF GUYANA'S NATIONALIST MOVEMENT

In the Guyanese context, apart from the legacy of
racial snobbery, injustice, blatant inequalities and
severed reference group ties, evidence of social disorganization, relative deprivation and alienation at various
levels of the colonial society were poignant factors that
catalysized the surg of nationalist movements with standardized negative attitudes towards the colonialists.
The significance of socio-cultural disorganization
and alienation as a basic variable in the rise and growth
of Guyana's Nationalist movement is apparent during the
nineteenth and early twentieth centuries, when the
Colonialists reinforced their social, economic, and
political positions through a series of special privileges.
They (the colonialists) "were elevated to a position of power
from which they shaped colonial policy to suit their own
interest" (Despres, 1967, p. 42). Concomitantly, the
colonialists were reluctant to entrust responsibility
to Guyanese, and maintained a monopoly of the major
institutions. Too much consideration was given to the
popular belief that they (the colonialists) knew what
was best for the subjected people. This lack of participation
on the part of the Guyanese in institutions of real

consequence created alienation of Guyanese from the major social structures. Peter Simms (1966) refers to this "rule of privilege" as one of the worst aspects of British rule, particularly as it closed the doors to well-qualified Guyanese. Over a period of time, such processes of socio-cultural disorganization and alienation led to a sense of collective frustration, of inferiority, uselessness and powerlessness among those who were making serious efforts to improve their lot.

In the eyes of Guyanese, the most agonizing contradiction of the colonial situation was the readiness of its proponents to suggest that the system of "rule of privilege" contributed greatly to their well being. As Sherif and Sherif (1969) point out "humans - be they white, yellow, or black - do not judge what they are and what they have and what they do in absolute terms, but in relation to others - especially if the others have assumed an air of superoirity, with special privileges and claims of dominance, and practised their dominance by brute force and laws they imposed for decades" (p.530). The relative nature of participation in the political process can be best illistrated in the electorate and civil service.

Table 1. Composition of Electorate in 1915 +

Race	Percentage of Each Race in Adult Male Population	Percentate of Each Race in Total Elector- ate (N4, 312)	Percentahe of Adult Males of Each Race Regis tered as Voters
East Indian	51.8	6.4	0.6
African	42.3	62.7	6.8
Portuguese	2.9	11.4	17.7
British	1.7	17.0	46.1
Chinese	0.9	2.4	12.3

Source: + Despres, L., Cultural Pluralism and Nationalist Politics in British Guiana, P.40.

As Table 1 indicates, until 1915, the colonialists held an inordinate proportion of positions in the political system despite their being a minority group in the population. This situation persisted - with minor constitutional reform-until 1953 when constitutional advancement called for open elections on the basis of universal adult suffrage. Granted that under the constitution that existed at that time (1915), the vote meant very little. However, the composition of the electorate is indicative of the relative positions which various cultural groups had come to occupy within the European-dominated power structure (Despres, 1969, pp. 39-40).

Figures in Table 2 indicate all but seven of the thirty-four executive heads of the civil service departments were held by Colonialists with the philosophy of the "whiteman's burden" created a threat to the self-image and self-reliance of the Guyanese people. Furthermore, the pitiful gap that existed between whites and non-whites in institutions of real consequence during several successive decades was defined by the Guyanese value system as intolerable and not a proper condition of life. This resentment was well expressed by Smith (1962) when he stated that "the simple fact is that many Guyanese would like to run their own affairs even if they ran them somewhat less effieiently, or even downright badly" (pp. 85 - 86).

Table 2. Ethnic Composition of Department of
Executive Heads of Civil Servants in 1940

Ethnic Composition	Departmental or Executive Heads	Percent
European	27	79.4
Afro Guyanese	5	14.7
East Indians	0	0.0
Portuguese	2	5.9
Chinese and others	0	0.0
Total	34	100.0

Source: ++ Ibid. p. 163.

This cursory description of the colonial situation and the growth of the nationalist movement in Guyana remains inadequate without mentioning the economic domination suffered by Guyanese. At the economic level, Guyanese were denied the right of full participation in and control over their own economic affairs. Employment policies based on particularistic and ascriptive criteria were widespread among the commercial and indistrial institutions (Despres, 1967, Newman 1964). Until recently, all top levels in the corporate structure were composed of British and Canadian personnel, although these cultural groupongs comprised only 2.5 percent of the inhabitants (Mitchell, et al., 1969). Intentionally, or not, the colonialists promoted the exclusion of Guyanese from full participation in higher levels of decision-making processes. The impression was that the colonialists were not concerned with rightness but rather with whiteness.

Closely interwoven with alienation and socio-cultural disorganization was the control of the mass media by the colonialists. The super power used the mass media to "emphasize the social, economic and cultural values attached to British colonial ties" (Despres 1967, p. 133). To compound the tragedy further, early traditional leaders of Guyana formed a coalition with the Colonialists to perpetuate and preserve the status quo (Newman 1964).

EMERGENCE OF A COMPREHENSIVE IDENTITY

When one considers the type of phenomena outlined above, it becomes quite apparent that for some time Guyanese were shackled by severe alienation and socio-cultural disorganization. From a social psychological point of view, alienation and socio-cultural disorganization are stimulated by disruption of reference group ties and erosion of stable ego-anchorages.

Disruption of reference group ties implies that the alienated person has lost his social and psychological support and that the existing standards and norms no longer serve as dependable guides to action. Caught up in such personal uncertainty and insecurity, the

individual tends to become anomic. The consequences of
this situation becomes psychologically painful to the
individual and arouses striving to resurrect his old
ties or to search for new ones. In time, individuals
facing the same predicament tend to band together in
the collective quest of restructuring of reference
group ties and finding a satisfying stable ego-identity.
For example, Black Power emerged in the U.S.A. to
develop an identity for Afro-Americans. African nationalism arose to revive African self-respect. Nazism
emerged to reassert Aryan identity. Similarly, in
Guyana, nationalism flourished to reassert a new sense
of pride and pooled self-esteem. In time, new norms
and values are developed through the process of patterned
collective interaction, and the individuals involved
form new conceptions of themselves with standardized
negative attitudes towards the oppressor.

In essence, the cumulative results of alienation,
socio-cultural disorganization and snapped reference
group ties, together with their social and psychological
consequences, provided the background from which emerged
social cohesion and a significantly comprehensive
nationalist movement for self determination. The
sentiments of frustration, alienation and self-determination coalesced and gave way to collective agitation.
As Mitchell and others put it:

> Individual frustration began to assume a new
> dimension as particulatistic interests were
> submerged by the larger national concerns,
> culminating in the emergence of a new sense
> of national identity. This essentially anti-
> colonial sentiment was most fully expressed
> in the fight for independence (p. 222)

The stimulus for the formation of a comprehensive
nationalist movement did not rest only on the matrix
of discontent. Several other specific factors provided
important incentive to the collective quest for self-
determination. Among these are considerable world
condemnation of colonialism after World War II; the

U.N. General Assembly resolution calling for immediate independence to all colonial territories; the coura-
geous struggle of peoples in Asia and Africa for their
independence; the emergence of a new working class and
its demands for more active participation in the
decision making process; constitutional advancement and
the return of western educated elites.

"Over and above other factors, it was the charismatic
leadership of a few men that caused modern nationalism
to flourish after World War II" (Rotberg 1966, p. 517).
Promoted by the motivational base outlined, the western
educated elites having a new set of values and goals
(a desire for material progress, justice, equality and
active participation in the decision-making process
rather than mere recipient of it) impregnated their
compatriots with the incipient sense of self assertion
through nationalism.

Paridoxically, in the post World War II period,
western educated elites have almost invariably provided the leadership of nationalist movements (Emerson
1960). The struggle of Guyana's political independence
was led primarily by a duo of charismatic leaders with
western education (Cheddi Jagan an American trained
dentist of East Indian descent and L.F.S. Burnham a
British trained lawyer of African descent). Mutual
dislike for the European-dominated structure cemented
the coalition between Afro-Guyanese and East Indian
intellectuals. Instead of being staunch defenders of
the status quo, the western educated elites openly
challenged the established power structure.

Perhaps these western educated elites provided the
leadership in the incipient nationalist movement
because:

1. during their studies and travels abroad
they came into contact with a dominant culture that
awakened a desire for equality and freedom from the
super-imposition of "Englishness" on their way of life;

2. coming into contact with nationalists from other countries who were in the same predicament, these elites came to the realization that the time for change in the mode of government had come; and

3. on their return home, they were the most directly affected by the motivational base-most marginal and alienated from the established order. For example, upon returning home there were no effective demands for their skills and knowledge in institutions of real consequence, even though such was needed. Positions of responsibility were reserved only for the colonialists.

TRENDS TOWARD COORDINATION OF THE NATIONALIST MOVEMENT

In Guyana, doors were closed to Guyana's intelligentsia in positions of real consequence, regardless of whether they were better qualified than the Englishmen performing the same jobs (Peter Simms 1966). This policy of keeping Guyana's intelligentsia "in their place" created disruption of refernece group ties and loss of stable ego-anchorages. This state of stress and strain manifested itself in many ways. Some alienated elites sought stable ego identity by entering a coalition with the established power structure, while others, refusing to accept the non-realization of their values and goals, threw in their lot with the rank and file in search of their ego-stability. Or, as Sherif and Sherif (1969) put it, "To lack a sense of belongingness, to feel isolated from people around one, to see little or nothing left to hang on to, arouses strivings to restore one's ties or to re-establish new bearings" (p. 421).

Thus, many of the alienated elites were convinced that the only way to rediscover their ego-stability was to pattern their interaction collectively through the nationalist movement. Refusing to accept the obstacles in the colonial setting which constantly thwarted their efforts for self-realization, the western educated elites for the first time openly challenged the established power structure. Subsequently, the early 1950's saw the emergence of a

comprehensive nationalist movememt. The alienated
elites formed the nucleus of the comprehensive nationalist movement and manifested itself as the bi-racial
People's Progressive Party (P.P.P.) - through which
collective striving for national identity and self
determination gravitated (Mitchell et al 1969, Despres
1967).

The emergence of an integrative nationalist front
was due in part to the need for coordinating the "Bill
of gripes" and to provide some effective means to a way
out of their common predicament (Sherif and Sherif 1969).
The integrative function of the nationalist party in
Guyana was manifested in two important ways. First,
it brought out a coalition of interest from peoples in
the same predicament, i.e. African and Indian masses
and elites. Secondly, it brought disparate socio-
cultural and political units towards a larger and
more inclusive unit. In referring to the comprehensive
nature of the People's Progressive Party, Decaires and
Fitzpatrick (1966) stated that:

> Racially, the party represented a step
> towards the unification of the African and
> Indian workers and intellectuals who shared
> in the common desire to remove the imperial
> presence and initiate a program of social
> reform.
>
> Economically, the party represented a coali-
> tion of peasant "rural proletarian" and city
> workers; all in different ways affected by
> the social structure of colonial rule and
> all eager for change (p. 39).

Viewed from certain vantage points, the People's
Progressive Party, as a comprehensive nationalist
movement, was forging towards a national identity
and unity. People in the movement rejected loyalties
of local scope for national commitment. "Sentiments
of national unity transcended race, class or religious
affiliation" (Smith 1962, p. 171). Similarly, as
Despres (1967) noted, the formation of a larger and

more inclusive organization - the P.P.P. - the party's ideological stance of interdependence among the units facing a common predicament, and the struggle for the right of the Guyanese people to exist free from alien domination; all contributed to a new definition of self and an enlarged sense of 'we-ness' among the party members. "For the first time in their history the Guyanese had something whereby they could perceive themselves as one people. Individual frustrations began to take on a sense of meaning within the framework of a national point of view" (Despres 1967, p.5). Evidence of this was borne out in the first election held under universal suffrage in 1953 when the P.P.P. captured 18 out of the 24 contested seats in the House of Assembly.

But, the formation of a more inclusive unit with goals directed towards change of the social order caused the organization of opposition forces because change on the power relations or perceived change meant the disruption of the established positions and interests of the colonialists. It was precisely at this stage of Guyanese solidarity that the opposition force - the Colonialists - moved to break the common front against them by instituting their proverbial policy of "divide and rule".

One hundred and thirty three days after the P.P.P. success at the polls, the colonialists demonstrated their heavy hand by suspending the constitution and removing from office the freely elected government under the guise of thwarting a communist takeover. By assigning the entire blame to Jagan and his left wing supporters and portraying Burnham and his right wing followers as a more moderate socialist group, the colonialists were successful in imposing strain and mutual distrust between the Jaganite and Burnhamite factions of the P.P.P. In fact, for preservation of the status quo, the colonialists were exploiting racial differences and also attempting to supress nationalist movements toward self-determination.

CRISIS IN LEADERSHIP AND RISE OF FACTIONALISM

The crisis between the leaders of Guyana's comprehensive nationalist movement arose in part because of long standing disagreement on strategy for clear cut action for achievement of independence. Mututal distrust between the left and right wing factions of the P.P.P. intensified the struggle for political power between the leaders.

Thus, in 1955, when the split occurred bringing about two competing factions namely the Burnhamites and Jaganites, the comprehensive nationalist movement for independence had disintegrated into the politics of race.

This kind of jockeying for power might have been natural after independence was won,+ but it occurred at a time when it was percieved by the Burnhamite faction that Jagan would not be permitted by the Colonialists to take office. Burnham was seen as the one who would organize his followers under a more moderate platform.

The factions that emerged fell along lines of racial identity and party affiliation. This development awakened latent fears of racial animosities between the Jaganite faction retaining the name People's Progressive Party or P.P.P. and consisting predominantly of East Indian followers, and the Burnhamite faction - later renamed People's National Congress and consisting predominantly of African followers.

+Sherif (1966, p. 169) argues that prior to independence the mutual dislike for the oppressor is a core aspect that cemented the unity of an oppressed people. However, once independence is achieved, the common tie of opposition towards the oppressor is no longer sufficient to provide common bonds for national unity.

The very structure and the nature of the factions and
their leadership did not allow for solution of problems
of the people in national terms but rather in terms that
benefited their group. (Carter, 1965). People began
to be increasingly aware of their ethnic identity and
tended as a result of political mobilization to view
various issues and situations not according to national
priorities but rather according to their genealogical
background.

The manifestation of the politics of "apanjaht" -
vote for your race - was evident in the 1957 and 1961
general elections which Jagan (P.P.P.) won. In 1957
the Jagan faction polled 47.5 percent of the total
vote and Burnhamis faction 25.5 percent. The two
other registered parties, the United Democratic Party
and the National Labor Front together polled 19.7
percent. In 1961 elections the P.P.P. won 46.7 percent,
P.N.C. 44.7 percent and United Force (U.F. - a new
party consisting of conservative businessmen with a
long history of colonial ties) polled 8.3 percent. These
results closely resembled the racial composition of
Guyana's East Indian, Black and Mixed population.

In carrying out "apanjaht" policies, Jagan designed
his development program to benefit the East Indians in
order to solidify his support. A major portion of the
G$40 million program went towards land development
(benefited predominantly by East Indians), and rapid
promotion and infusion of East Indians into the Civil
Service was the order of the day.

The newly formed political party, United Force (U.F.)
led by Peter D'Aguiar sought to protect the interests
of the owners of businesses, mostly those of Portuguese
descent, and other Europeans. This party consisted of
those who were clearly the colonialists and by its
existence contributed to the racial and political conflicts.

Thus, the leaders and the political structures with
which they were working aggravated racial conflict -

143

evident in civil disorders from 1962 through 1964.

In 1966, Guyana became independent from Britain under a coalition Government of P.N.C. and U.F. led by L.F.S. Burnham.

Despite the fact that under the leadership of Burnham, Guyana has gone a long way in strengthening the relations between the cultural groups, ethnic rivalries are still alive and well and are manifested in racial and political conflicts. These conflicts are very real and have the effect of disrupting what an independent nation should be striving to attain by diverting some of the energies to obtaining and maintaining power. In this state of affairs, the leaders of the factions and their rank and file are making no serious efforts towards reaching some consensus for an integrated society.

By the time elections were held in 1968, the P.N.C./ U.F. coalition had collapsed. Burnham won a majority of the seats though the election was accompanied by a violent controversy over allegations of vote rigging and allowing Guyanese living in other countries to register a vote.

The succeeding years saw the birth of pressure groups such as: The Movement Against Oppression (M.A.O.), the Fundamenta Rights Action Committee (F.R.A.C.) and the African Society for Cultural Relations with Independent Africa (A.S.C.R.I.A.). These groups could well mold the future political pattern of Guyana, particularly in the effort to move the country toward a one party state.

During the drive of the comprehensive nationalist movement and thereafter, a popular cry loudly echoed was "Backra day done", meaning the white man's day is over. However, looking at present conditions one tends to question this assertion. The factors that shaped the colonial society prior to independence are still there, i.e. the colonial structure of the society, over-domination of the economy by foreign investment, and racial and political disharmony etc.

Sugar is still king in Guyana despite the efforts by the government to reduce sugar as a corner stone of the economy. Today, sugar accounts for over 40 percent of the total value of all exports. This portion of the economy affects directly or indirectly 80 percent of the population. Moreover, despite Guyanization on sugar estates - introducing local persons into decision-making positions - the structure of the society changed very little. A disproportionate number of colonial-ists are still at the managerial level with the locals occupying the intermediate and bottom of the social scale.

The government hopes to develop a system of co-opera-tivism involving peasant cane farmers etc. and later move inte processing and manufacturing. A co-operative state, at the moment, exists only as an ideal. It is intended to be an instrument of the "small man" to own part of the economy the thereby to raise his level of living. But if someone else controls the strings to the purse then Guyanese people will never be master of their own destinies. It appears that the Guyanese people, once owned by the colonialists as slaves or indentured workers, are now rented by them.

The successful integration of various ethnic groups still remains a problem. The slogan of independence "out of many, one people" is still a far cry from reality. The racial and political animosities, though played down by the Burnham government are still ever present.

CONCLUSION

This paper is not intended to create the illusion that nationalist movements and factionalism are merely journeys into the wilderness in search of a stable identity. Nationalist movements seek the eradication of social injustices, inequalities, deprivations, frustrations, etc., while forging towards a stable identity through psychological bonds at the national level.

It is unfortunate that Guyana is divided along racial cultural and political lines. As Decaries and Fitzpatrick (1966) put it, "Not only does Guyana remain divided but influences within the society are directed to emphasize the factors which separate the people rather than those which unite them (p. 44).

Inasmuch as independence has been achieved, racial disharmony and the accompanying mistrust created by the growth of factionalism seriously impedes internal and external advances.

The solution to this problem must go beyond providing a few jobs for a few people, building a few roads and increasing the police force. The Guyana Government must go beyond just being overseer of its economy, and be owner of it. Steps in this direction were recently followed when the Government nationalized the Demerara Bauxite Company. The major culprit - British owned sugar industry - is as yet untouched.

A massive attack on unemployment which is at present over 20 percent of the labor force, is needed. Avenues for mobility, lacking in the present plantation structure of the society must be created. Most importantly, maneuvering the Indo-Guyanese (the majority of the people with a higher rate of natural increase than other groups) onto a minority role in the government by a continued coalition of other groups and by other political moves will not bring about the racial climate necessary for cooperation.

BIBLIOGRAPHY

Burnham, Forbes, Foreword to Journal of New World. Georgetown: New World Group Associates, 1966.

Carter, Martin, "The Race Crisis in Guiana" in Irving Pflaum Journal of the Caribbean Institute and Study for Latin America. San German Puerto Rico: Inter American University Press, 1965

Decaires, David and Fitzpatrick, Miles, "Twenty Years of Politics in Our Land" in George Lamming and Martin Carter (eds) Journal of New World. Georgetown: New World Group Associates, 1966.

Despres, Leo, A., Cultural Pluralism and Nationalist Politics in British Guiana, Chicago: Rand McNally and Co., 1967.

Emerson, R., From Empire to Nation. Cambridge: Harvard University Press, 1960.

King, Sidney, "A Birth of Freedom" in George Lamming and Martin Carter (eds) Journal of New World. Georgetown: New World Group Associates, 1966.

Mitchell, William B. and others, Area Handbook for Guyana. Washington: U.S. Government Printing Office, 1969.

Newman, Peter, British Guiana Problems of Cohesion in an Immigrant Society. London: Oxford University Press, 1964.

Rotberg, R.I., "The Rise of African Nationalism: The Case of East and Central Afroca" in Immanuel Wallerstein (ed) Social Change: The Colonial Situation. New York: John Wiley and Sons, Inc., 1966.

Sherif, Muzafer and Sherif, Carolyn, Social Psychology. New York: Harper and Row Publishers, 1969.

Sherif, Muzafer, In Common Predicament. Boston: Houghton Mifflin Co., 1966

Simms, Peter, Trouble in Guiana. London: George Allen and Unwin Ltd.,1966.

Smith, Raymond T., British Guiana. London: Oxford University Press, 1962.

BAUXITE:
The Need to Nationalize, Part I

By Norman Girvan

I. Bauxite Nationalization

The case for national ownership and control of the Caribbean bauxite industry derives from the case against ownership and control by the multi-national aluminum companies. These companies utilize Caribbean bauxite to service their own needs of long-term growth and profitability. That is their prerogative, so long as they own the resource. Indeed it is their duty, for that is what they exist to do. But the pursuit of this objective leads to the systematic divorce of the bauxite resources of the Caribbean from the needs and objectives of the material development of the Caribbean people.

THE REVIEW OF BLACK POLITICAL ECONOMY, 1971, Vol. 2, No. 1, pp. 72-94.

A. The Typical Aluminum Firm

To illustrate this we need to understand the structure of the typical aluminum company which mines bauxite in the Caribbean. There are three outstanding characteristics that one must know in order to understand how these firms function and how they affect the Caribbean bauxite industry. First, the typical firm is *vertically integrated.* This means that bauxite mines in the Caribbean are geared to provide the raw material feed for specific alumina plants owned by the company, whether the plant is in the Caribbean or in North America. It means that the alumina plants are in turn geared specifically to provide the plant feed for aluminum smelters, which are in turn geared to fabricating plants. Often, the other supplies required by the plants, such as caustic and electric power, are also produced by plants owned by the company.

The second important characteristic is that the typical firm is *multi-product.* This means that besides its main product line — aluminum — it is also engaged in the production of other goods and services. Usually, these are goods or services which are related to aluminum in some way, such as chemicals, refractories or electric power.

The third important characteristic is that the typical firm is *multinational.* It is engaged in its many activities in a large number of countries. Thus the typical aluminum firm mines bauxite in a number of different Caribbean countries and elsewhere in the world, carries out alumina, aluminum production and fabrication in Europe, Africa, Asia and Oceania as well. We should, however, note that the term *multinational* refers to the *geographic* spread of the company's activities and not to the locus of decision-making. Fundamental, long-term decision-making concerning the strategy of the firm's growth is centralized at a clearly identifiable head office, although *operational* decisions are decentralized to the level of the division, the department or the plant.

These three characteristics give rise to the *large sizes* of the firms, the characteristic which is most visible and most well known to Caribbean people.

A good way to illustrate these characteristics in concrete terms is to take one of the bauxite companies operating in Guyana and follow the lines of its connections with the outside world. The Demerara Bauxite Company is a wholly-owned subsidiary of the Aluminium Company of Canada (Alcan) which is in turn a wholly-owned subsidiary of Alcan Aluminium Ltd. This last company is a holding company with operating subsidiaries and affiliates in thirty-three countries. Guyanese bauxite is made into alumina partly in Mackenzie and partly in Arvida at the alumina plant of Aluminium Ltd. of Canada. This alumina finds its way to the Arvida smelter, or possibly to the smelter of a Norwegian affiliate, A/S Norsk Aluminium Company. From there it might be shipped to Britain to be extruded into aluminum wire at the plant of Alcan Wire Ltd. or it might even find its way into the economy of *apartheid,* through the plants of Alcan Aluminium of South Africa Ltd.

The company's assets at the end of 1968 were valued at $2,150 million of which only $279 million were in the Caribbean and South America, $1,212 million in North America, $390 million in the United Kingdom and continental Europe and $269 million in the rest of the world. Total revenues in that year were $1,346 million, profits $86 million and cash provisions for depreciation and depletion $87 million. The entire corporate domain is planned and overseen from headquarters in Montreal, under the presidency of Nathaniel K. Davis. Guyanese bauxite and alumina production falls under the portfolio of Donald Mackay, executive vice-president in charge of raw materials. Mr. Mackay is therefore Alcan's Minister of Bauxite. Other vice-presidents have responsibility for finance, smelting, fabricating and sales, and legal affairs.

The other large North American companies — Reynolds, Alcoa and Kaiser — are basically similar in structure, size and administration.

B. Effects of the Multinational Firm on Caribbean Bauxite Industry

The features of the aluminum firms mean that the bauxite reserves under their control are utilized for their own growth and development, and at the same time divorced from the growth and development of Caribbean countries. It needs to be emphasized that this is not a result of the "bad" policies of "bad" firms. To be sure, the managements of Alcoa, Alcan, Reynolds and Kaiser would like to be in a position to feel that the operations of their companies lead to the economic development of Jamaica, Guyana and Surinam so long as this is consistent with their business strategy. The trouble is that it is not. This can be illustrated with reference to the pricing and processing of bauxite, and the use of profits from the industry.

Very little of the bauxite or alumina produced in the Caribbean is actually "sold" to anyone. Most of it is shipped to the alumina or aluminum plants of the parent companies which produce it. The price is set by the parent company according to whether it wants its profit to appear in its bauxite operation, or its alumina, or aluminum or shipping operation. *All* vertically-integrated firms do this. It is part of the way in which they maximize profits. And in spite of the energetic efforts of the governments of Guyana, Surinam and Jamaica over the last twenty years, they continue to be at the mercy of the companies in regard to the prices used for ordinary bauxite, calcined, chemical and abrasive-grade bauxite, alumina, and aluminum. As a result, large amounts of taxes have not been paid to the Caribbean people.

There is ultimately no way in which just pricing can be assured—from our point of view—unless and until the Caribbean people own the products which are being sold.

However, the important effects possible from bauxite lie not so much in obtaining tax revenues as in using the material as a basis for a large-scale industrial complex. The Caribbean can appreciate this at a glance by noting the enormous assets and revenues of the aluminum companies which obtain most of their bauxite from the Caribbean. Most of these assets and revenues are based on the use of Caribbean bauxite. In transforming a ton of bauxite into semi-fabricated aluminum, the value rises from between $14 and $28 to somewhere in the region of $350. On the Caribbean output of about 17 million tons of bauxite the value of semi-fabricated aluminum output resulting is in the region of $6,000 million. By far, the bulk of this represents the income of workers, shareholders, and governments in the United States, Canada and the rest of the world. Some of this is produced directly by the processes of transforming the bauxite, and some in the industries which sell supplies to the aluminum industry, such as electric power, petroleum, chemicals and transport. Hence, just as in the times of the slave trade and indentured labor, the Caribbean continues to make a massive contribution to metropolitan economic development.

It is obvious that the Caribbean does not intend to allow this to continue any longer, and that it shall instead ensure that bauxite contributes to its own development. It is equally clear that to ensure this the Caribbean shall have to own and control the industry, so that is shall decide how its bauxite will be used.

This ties up with the question of the use of profits in the industry. The profits earned from bauxite production in the Caribbean are quite substantial in relation to the total income of the Caribbean, especially if it uses just prices to value this production. And the profits earned from the production of alumina, aluminum and semi-fabricated aluminum are fantastic. The profits earned by the four large aluminum companies in 1968, before deducting taxes and depreciation, amounted to $1,488 million.

From the Caribbean point of view, the profits earned from bauxite production should be used to set up alumina production, those earned from alumina should be used to set up aluminum, and so on. The profits from the entire industry should be used partly for expanding it within the Caribbean, and partly to finance the development of other sectors of the Caribbean economy, such as agriculture and education. But at present these profits are used to finance the development of the *companies'* economies. And this means the expansion of aluminum and semi-fabricated production in North America and elsewhere in the developed world.

This means that the Caribbean will have to own the industry if it is to use the profits for its own development, to give itself the chance to bring food, clothes, housing and education to all Caribbean people.

C. Why Nationalize?

There are many people who recognize that the Caribbean is getting a "bad deal" out of bauxite, and who feel that it ought to get a "better deal." They argue, quite sincerely, that nationalization would bring problems that the Caribbean could not handle, and that it should instead concentrate its efforts on getting improvements from the companies such as higher taxes, and more alumina and aluminum plants within the Caribbean.

The trouble with this strategy is that it does not allow for Caribbean *control* over the industry, and control is the most important factor. Take the question of taxes. It might be quite possible to get the companies to pay more taxes on their production here. But the factors which *determine* taxes—such as prices and deductible costs—would still be under the control of the companies. And once it begins to consider deciding for itself what prices shall rule, it is beginning to talk about control.

Or take the more important question of processing. It might be possible to get the companies to build more alumina plants in the Caribbean, and even to put up the odd aluminum smelter here and there. Some governments have succeeded in getting them to do this. But the companies will still be in a position to decide, on the bases of their world-wide resources and opportunities, where the processing of Caribbean bauxite will take place. In the past, these decisions have led to the bulk of processing being done abroad, and there is little reason to believe that this will change fundamentally in the future.

In fact, the future holds some real mysteries for the Caribbean as far as the companies' policies are concerned. This is partly the result of possible new technologies. One process now being developed by the companies reduces aluminum directly from bauxite, and eliminates the alumina stage altogether. If this comes into wide commercial use, the Caribbean will no longer be able to bargain for alumina plants, but will have the more difficult task of bargaining for new-type aluminum plants. Another process which is technically feasible, but not yet cheap, extracts alumina from clays found widely in the United States. If this comes into wide commercial use, then the Caribbean will no longer be able to use its possession of bauxite as a basis for bargaining for alumina and aluminum plants. The Caribbean people can see, then, why it is essential and urgent for them to be in a position to make their own decisions in the industry, and develop their own technologies.

Finally, so long as they do not own the industry, they will not be in a position to earn the massive profits which flow from it. And they cannot get these profits through taxation, for as soon as they begin to tax away most of these profits, they can be sure that the companies will stop investing in local expansion, and these companies might even go so far as to reduce production.

II. How to Nationalize

A. The Objective of Nationalization

The Caribbean government which takes the basic decision to

nationalize needs to have its objectives very clearly established before embarking on the process. This is because such a decision will certainly bring enormous opposing pressures, from the companies, from 'their home governments, and possibly too, from internal political forces. The danger represented by these pressures is not only that they might "persuade" the government to abandon the goal of nationalization in return for an inferior substitute. It is also that they might successfully pressure the government to accept the form of nationalization without the content. Recent nationalizations indeed demonstrate that this latter possibility is as real as the first one.

It might be best, therefore, to make explicit the objectives of nationalization which were implicit in the preceding analysis. The Caribbean needs to nationalize in order to secure *effective* national ownership over the industry; and *effective* control over decision-making, especially in regard to pricing and marketing, the purchase of supplies, processing and expansion, and the use of profits.

B. *Previous Nationalization Experiences*

Every sovereign government has the right to nationalize. But the people of the Caribbean know that this counts for very little in a world where military and economic power is loaded heavily on the side of the companies and countries from which they seek to recover their natural resources. So it would be useful for them to consider briefly the experience of other countries in the Third World which have nationalized large, metropolitan companies, especially mining companies. They need to know how these countries went about nationalization, what difficulties they encountered, and what factors contributed to their success or failure in overcoming these difficulties. The cases which can be of assistance to us are the following: the Mexican oil nationalization of 1938, the Persian oil nationalization of 1952, Egypt's nationalization of Suez in 1956, the Cuban nationalizations of 1960, the Peruvian oil nationalization of 1968, Chilean and Zambian copper nationalization in 1969, and the 1969 joint venture between Guinea and a number of aluminum companies. (The last-named involves a national share ownership of 49 percent only, but the experience is still of value.)

The conclusions arising out of these experiences can be grouped into six main categories, relating to:

(1) payment for the nationalized assets, (2) management and operation of the nationalized facilities, (3) marketing of the nationalized output, (4) the degree and nature of opposition by the parent companies, (5) the degree and nature of the opposition of the foreign governments concerned, and (6) the factors involved in the relative success of the nationalizing government in overcoming this opposition.

Payment. The most important questions concern the valuation of the nationalized assets and the speed with which payment is made. At one end of the spectrum, payment may be withheld altogether. This has happened in cases where nationalization was partly or wholly an act of retaliation in a dispute between the government and the companies, or their own home governments. Thus Cuba has withheld payment for nationalized American property pending restoration of the United States sugar quota and Peru has withheld payment for the assets of the International Petroleum Company pending settlement of her claims for back taxes which exceed the value of the nationalized assets many times over.

At the other end of the spectrum payment may be made immediately, in convertible cash, on the basis of the market value of the assets. Hence, Chile paid for its 51 percent share in the assets of Kennecot's subsidiary within two years, in dollars, and on a market valuation which was more than double the book value.

Obviously the first examples noted imply government ownership with no cash outlay whatever, and the second implies almost immediate cash outlays in terms of foreign currency. Conversely, the first examples involve no cash receipts for the firm and the second involves almost immediate receipts in convertible currency. What locates the position of any given case in the spectrum — from the "capture" to the "purchase" position — depends on four factors: (a) the basis of the valuation of the assets, (b) the currency in which payment is made, (c) the length of time over which payment is stretched, and (d) the rate of interest paid on the value of the assets not yet paid for.

Valuation can be, by and large, the book value, the replacement value or the market value. The book value is simply the sum of all the historical costs of the fixed assets in place, minus the amounts historically for depreciation of these assets. Current assets such as supplies and inventories, at cost, and working capital, will of course be included. Replacement value is based on how much it would cost the firm to replace these assets. Since the cost of capital goods is always rising, and since they are bought before depreciation is deducted, replacement value will be significantly higher than book value. Market value is based on the estimated profitability of the assets over a period of time, after reducing these estimated future profits by an amount which represents the fact that future income is worth less than current income. As long as business conditions are reasonably good, market value will be the highest value of all. Hence it is least favorable to the country and most favorable to the company.

Payment can be made either in local currency or in foreign currency. If in local currency, and the local currency is fully convertible into foreign currency, then the effect is the same as if payment is made in foreign currency. The payment becomes a charge on the foreign exchange reserves and the foreign exchange earnings of the country. If the local currency is not convertible, however, and the government decides not to allow conversion into foreign currency for this payment, then the effect is to force the companies to take payment only in the form of locally available goods and services. They must first spend the money received within the country and then ship abroad the goods thus purchased for use or resale. Obviously this is least favorable to the company and most favorable to the country.

Payment can be made over a long or short period of time, and with a relatively low or high rate of interest on the unpaid portions. The instrument usually utilized to effect this is the special issue of government bonds to the companies to the value of the assets, however determined. The terms of the issue will specify when the bonds will be redeemed by the government, and the rate of interest, as well as the currency in which interest and principal will be paid. Thus, for example, the Zambian government paid for its 51 percent share in the copper mines with 8-year negotiable government bonds, bearing 6 percent interest, both principal and interest payable in United States dollars. Valuation was at book value. These terms are relatively favorable to the companies, for governments have in other cases used 20-year non-negotiable bonds at 5 percent interest, on the basis of book value. Obviously the longer the time period of payment and the lower the interest rate used, the more favorable are the terms to the government and the less so to the companies, and vice versa.

Management and Operation. Since the industries have been run with foreign management, technology and equipment, all nationalizing governments have had to face the problem of keeping production going in the short run, and mastering all aspects of the industry necessary for long run growth and expansion. The experiences suggest that where nationalization takes place over the bitter opposition of the companies, they withdraw foreign management and technical personnel, thus provoking serious short run problems. Yet these cases—Mexico, Egypt, Cuba—also show that after the inevitable initial period of dislocation, and trial and error, the shock of the withdrawal actually acts as a stimulus for the rapid development of indigenous managerial and technical skills and the production of indigenous technical equipment. And, as a result of this, the country emerges with a feeling of confidence in its own abilities which it never had before. This is an intangible but nonetheless indispensable psychological asset in the process of economic and cultural development. Thus the countries which have been prepared to pay the necessary price of this course, in terms of a few years' dislocation, have usually found the returns well worth the costs.

Countries which *negotiated* nationalization, however, such as Chile and Zambia, have opted to allow the companies continued operational control through management contracts. This means that the act of nationalization is a financial transaction dealing with the transfer of shares, but life in the mines continues as before. This arrangement has appealed to the governments because it ensures uninterrupted smooth operations of the facilities and a continued smooth flow of revenues from the industry into the government's coffers. It also appeals to the inferiority complex which most Third World governments feel with respect to their ability to run large, foreign-owned industries.

Another reason for this arrangement is that the companies demand it as part of their price for negotiating nationalization. Management contracts are good business, since they are paid for on a commission basis based on a percentage of revenue. Just as important, they leave effective operational control in the hands of the companies, thereby making it possible for them to continue to utilize the operation as part of a world-wide system of corporate control. Hence the Zambianization of 1969 was almost certainly anticipated and planned for by the companies.

Over a year before the move, the comment was made in a book published by the Economist Intelligence Unit in London (a kind of business information service) that in Zambia

> a Government take-over by around 1975 might reasonably be expected. This is probably the sort of target which the companies themselves would accept, and they might well co-operate with the Government in reaching it. The companies might, however, seek to retain participation in the Zambian industry, particularly in smelting and refining, and might also seek to keep control over export marketing of copper.[1]

The irony is that both Chile and Zambia have pointed proudly to the management contracts as one of the "achievements" of the nationalization packets rather than viewing them as concessions. It is true that the relationships between the managing companies and the boards of directors on which the governments have a majority, have not become clearly established. But there is no doubt about the companies' intention to exercise continued control as far as possible. Speaking at a Conference of Industrialists and Financiers sponsored by the United Nations Economic Commission for Africa in January, 1967, a vice-president of the Chase Manhattan Bank noted in relation to joint ventures that "the important element is that there be a meeting of minds at the beginning as to who does what—who manages and controls."[2] Under these circumstances, a minority shareholder can in fact not only manage but also control the enterprise.

Marketing. Since the companies themselves normally control export marketing outlets (often they are themselves the buyers of the commodity), and since the principal markets are normally found in the same metropolitan countries where they are based, the question of export marketing of nationalized output has always been a crucial one. A country might get around the problem simply by allowing the companies to continue marketing on a commission basis, as in the Zambian case and also in the case of the Congo. In both cases, the marketing contracts were parts of an over-all negotiated package deal which included a management contract and an agreed method of compensation.

The marketing contract is a device of relatively recent vintage and is yet another example of how the companies have learned to live with nationalization by turning a bad situation into a good one. In a number of other cases the nationalizing country has been forced to cope with the problem of marketing in the face of a boycott by the former companies and countries. The cases of Mexico, Persia, Cuba and Peru are examples.

In the Persian case, it was the failure to find markets for the nationalized oil which contributed to the collapse of the nationalizing regime and the eventual reversal of the nationalization. Mexico, Cuba and Peru did not end this way. Mexico was able partially to break the boycott because of the world-wide scarcity of oil induced by the outbreak of World War II. In the meantime, the new national oil company energetically established an extensive internal network of transport and distribution facilities, something which the foreign oil companies had neglected. This, and Mexico's rapid industrial growth, enormously stimulated domestic consumption of oil, with the result that by the 1950's the domestic market was absorbing the bulk of domestic oil output. In the Peruvian case most of the oil was already being sold locally; therefore, there was no real marketing problem. In the Cuban case, a political and economic alliance was cemented with a different metropolitan country, which has apparently been willing to let imports of the nationalized commodity grow at the expense of domestic production.

The results of the experience therefore suggest the following. The most desirable and most certain answer to the problem of export marketing is simply the domestic market—if actual or potential domestic consumption make this feasible. If this is not feasible, the two broad alternatives seem to be either a marketing contract with the former owners, as part of a total negotiated package deal, or an economic-political alliance with an entirely new country-customer.

There is, however, another real possibility which has not yet been put to a serious test, but which will have relevance to the nationalization of Caribbean bauxite. This is the possibility of playing different companies from different countries against one another such as United States companies against European countries. The companies are already doing this in their own way by playing one bauxite country against another, such as Guyana against Surinam.

The Intensity of Company Opposition. This is dependent on most of the factors already discussed — the valuation of assets, means payment, and degree of control left in the company's hands. The best deal for the companies is market valuation, paid for in hard currency in cash or short-term bonds, with management and marketing left in their control. A deal like that would be a windfall gain for many companies. Their opposition to nationalization can be expected to increase as any or all of these elements are altered in a less favorable direction.

There are three other factors that should be mentioned which determine the extent of company opposition. One is the rate of profit recovered from the operation before and after nationalization. *By bargaining for tax and exchange control concessions on their minority shareholding in the nationalized firm, companies have been able to use 51 percent nationalization as a means of recovering more profits from the operation.* This is precisely what happened with the Chileanization of Kennecot's subsidiary, and with Zambianization, and it helps explain why the companies agreed to the arrangements "voluntarily and enthusiastically," to use Kennecot's words.

The other factor relates to the importance of the nationalized assets to the profitability of the firm as a whole, both directly and indirectly. Where the assets in question represent a major part of the firm's assets, or where they represent access to raw materials upon which rests a major part of the global manufacturing and marketing position of the firm, one can expect company opposition to nationalization to be much greater than otherwise. Hence Anaconda, which draws from Chile only a small part of its copper. Similarly, the expropriation of its Peruvian subsidiary caused far less consternation to Esso than would the nationalization, say, of its Venezuelan subsidiary.

Of course this can work the other way as well. *Once a company is convinced that nationalization is inevitable,* it might be more willing to negotiate reasonably, the greater and the more strategic the assets at stake. In other words, since it is more vulnerable it might well be more reasonable. One of the reasons why Esso was so unreasonable, arrogant and insensitive in its dealings with Peru was probably that only a relatively small share of its operations was involved in the dispute.

The final factor which apparently determines the degree of

company opposition is the extent to which the company is able to mobilize the political, economic and military support of its home government, in the event of an open dispute with the nationalizing government.

Intensity and Nature of Foreign Government Opposition. Metropolitan governments are of course tied up with metropolitan businesses, and an important part of the foreign policy of these governments is concerned with protecting and furthering the interests of the corporate system as a whole, and those of individual corporation. Therefore the Caribbean people know that in the nationalization process these governments utilize various pressures with the nationalizing governments on behalf of the companies. The interesting question is: what determines the intensity of the pressure in the spectrum from mild diplomatic pressure, to suspension of aid, to a total trade boycott, to military intervention? All these have happened in the past, and this past experience can be a guide.

The first part of the answer is that the foreign government's position is partly dependent on the treatment of the nationalized company. The more unhappy the company is about the treatment it gets, the more intense will be the government pressure. But, of course, the attitude of the company to the nationalization is itself partly dependent on its judgment of the support it can mobilize from its government. So the Caribbean people have to get an idea of what other factors determine the government's attitude.

One such factor will be the size and political importance of the company within the metropolitan political system. It seems that one reason why Esso was able to mobilize the initial support of the United States government when Peru nationalized its subsidiary, in spite of its small operation and the highly questionable legal basis of Esso's position, was its political weight. Esso is one of the largest companies in the United States (and in the world), and together with the rest of the oil lobby, has a lot of influence in the United States Congress and with any United States administration.

But there are factors which go beyond the company's own position and which concern the general economic and strategic interests of the metropolitan government. The first of these is the importance of the nationalized assets themselves to the vital interests of the government. When Persia nationalized oil, what brought such intense reaction was the fact that "Great"

Britain's single largest source of oil supplies had been severed at the source. And Egypt's reclamation of the Suez Canal removed a critical link in the chain of Anglo-French influence in the Middle East. Hence, the governments' concern went far beyond the narrow question of compensation.

Finally, there is the government's judgment of the wider geo-political significance of the nationalization. This is most clearly revealed in the United State's attitude to the Cuban nationalizations. Of course, it is natural that no metropolitan government would like to wake up one morning to find that it has lost $800 million of its foreign investments! Nonetheless, what preoccupied the United States was the fact that a country within its own traditional sphere of influence had been lost to the sphere of influence of its chief rival, and under its nose at that! In this case, military intervention was far more than an operation on behalf of the nationalized sugar and other companies.

Overcoming the Difficulties. Where nationalization takes place over the opposition of the companies and their governments, how have governments overcome the inevitable difficulties? The relevant considerations seem to be the following: the opportunities afforded by the international economic situation, the opportunities afforded by the international political situation, the extent to which there is a collective front of all countries in the industry, and finally and most importantly, the internal resilience of the nationalizing country.

The international economic situation might afford opportunities for selling nationalized output to new customers and buying supplies from new suppliers. Mexico's use of the opportunities provided by war for selling its nationalized oil has been noted. How far these opportunities exist depends partly on the relative scarcity of the commodity internationally. It also depends on the rapidity with which the companies can replace the nationalized output with new output from other sources, in the markets previously supplied by the nationalized output. If the nationalized output was relatively large in world supplies, stocks are relatively low and it takes time-consuming and costly investments to bring new supplies into production. Therefore, it will take some time to replace the nationalized output, and vice versa. The opportunities for selling nationalized output will also depend on the strength and extent of the international market connections of the parent of the nationalized company or companies, and the degree of solidarity between that company and its competitors in the same industry, in dealing with the nationalizing government.

The international political situation is, of course, tied up with the economic situation; for example, whether or not a nationalizing government can find new markets also depends largely on the attitude of governments of other countries which are potential customers. The most important opportunities possible here are those arising out of the competing interests of different metropolitan countries. Previously the chief competing blocs were the Western World and the Communist World, but in recent years these have given way to many more groups: the United States, Europe, Japan, the Soviet Union and China at the least can be distinguished. The opportunities possible to nationalizing governments are accordingly rising.

The above considerations may be summed up by saying that the opportunities available to the nationalizing country will depend on the *lack* of solidarity in the rest of the world among companies and countries. And conversely, the position of the nationalizing country will be stronger, the greater is the solidarity among countries in a similar position, and the greater the degree of *internal* solidarity in the face of external pressure. Oil-producing countries have been able to extract a greater and greater share of revenues from the oil companies and are now contemplating participation in these companies, largely because of the strong position afforded through the Organization of Petroleum Exporting Countries. And it was the solidarity afforded by the Organization of Copper Producing Countries which helped encourage Chile and Zambia in their nationalizations in 1969. By contrast, Cuba's difficulties were multiplied by the failure of other sugar producers to support the sugar nationalization.

The last and most critical factor is the degree of internal solidarity and internal resilience in the polity of the nationalizing country. Where there are sharp internal divisions over the nationalization, and the population has not been prepared for the difficulties associated with external pressure, then the nationalization is almost certain to fail. This is the lesson of the Persian case—Mossadegh, the Prime Minister who nationalized oil, ended up in jail. But the Mexican and Cuban nationalizations were marked by a high degree of internal commitment. On closer examination we find that the reason was that the nationalizations were *part of a general revolutionary movement to establish national control over resources and introduce a degree of internal social and economic equality*. The lesson, therefore, is plain to see.

C. The Nationalization Strategy for Bauxite

So far the basic objectives of bauxite nationalization have been established and some lessons have been distilled from the rich and colorful history of previous nationalizations in the Third World. The next step is to indicate what elements a nationalization strategy for bauxite in the Caribbean should include if it is to have a reasonable chance to be viable.

Each Caribbean government in its approach to nationalization will have to start by making an evaluation of the basic strength of its bargaining position in the world bauxite industry. The first criterion used in this evaluation is the proportion of world output and of known world reserves of bauxite it possesses. It should also take into account the chemical composition of its ore reserves and the extent to which the technology of specific alumina plants owned by the companies is specific to these ore reserves. These factors together will determine two things: how important its bauxite is to existing company-users, and how anxious new company-users would be to have access to the bauxite.

In this connection, the most striking fact that emerges is that a relatively small group of countries—Jamaica, Surinam, Guyana, Guinea and Australia—possess the bulk of world bauxite production and reserves outside of the Communist bloc; and further, that the countries which use the most bauxite—The United States, Europe, the Soviet Union and Japan—are all short of domestic bauxite and most of them rely extensively on imported bauxite or alumina. This situation is in striking contrast to the situation in petroleum and, to a lesser extent, in copper. Hence there would seem to be a good chance for an Organization of Bauxite Exporting Countries (OBEC) collectively to exercise a reasonable amount of bargaining power in relation to the major using countries. The basic aim of such an organization would be to facilitate a take-over by the participating countries of the production and marketing of their bauxite, processing it locally into alumina and aluminum as far as possible. The present aluminum companies would become more and more fabricating companies consuming the bauxite, alumina and aluminum produced by national companies in the Third World.

Of course the major bauxite-producing countries will not all reach the position of wanting to reserve production for national companies at the same time—some will reach that position ahead of others. In that case the nationalizing country will still have a basis for collaboration with other bauxite countries in an OBEC. For the very least that such an organization could aim at is an agreement on bauxite pricing, which would raise prices, and therefore profits and taxes, in the exporting countries. Thus the first step of a nationalizing country should be to attempt to act as a catalyst for the formation of an OBEC, with a minimum target of an agreement on the pricing of bauxite and its products, and an ultimate target of a change in the international distribution of ownership and the international division of processing, within the industry. Naturally, if all bauxite countries do not join at first, it is still better to have a few—or only two—than none at all. The three largest Caribbean bauxite producers alone—Jamaica, Surinam and Guyana—control a significant part of world output and reserves.

The next question to be considered by the nationalizing government is the degree of opposition and hostility it can expect from the metropolitan government concerned — in this case, the United States. Since bauxite is a strategic war material, and the Caribbean has traditionally been an area of exclusive American control supplying the bulk of American requirements, it is certain that the United States will be vitally interested in the outcome of any threatened change in the status of American interests. We should note that this concern will be as much, if not more, about the question of *access* to Caribbean bauxite supplies as about the narrower questions relating to the *financial* and *economic* aspects of the change, which will be of greater interest to the companies than to the government. Whereas this certainly increases the pressures which will be exerted on the nationalizing government—including possible military intervention—it also creates an interesting possibility. It is this. It may well be that the United States government might not resist a nationalization which in its totality is quite financially and economically favorable to the nationalizing government, so long as it gets in return an assurance of adequate supplies of Caribbean bauxite and bauxite products. Another advantage of this strategy from the Caribbean's point of view is that the question of export outlets for existing output would also be solved. One can envisage two major dangers in this strategy, however. One is that, to be assured of continued bauxite supplies, the metropolitan interests would probably want devices such as management or marketing contracts, which leave effective control in their hands. The other is that an arrangement of this kind would entail continued subjection to the influence of American wishes about the location of bauxite processing, especially the location of aluminum smelters. In regard to this second danger, though, it should be noted that all the countries which are major users of bauxite wish to locate smelting within their borders, so that the Caribbean will have the bargaining problem in any case.

The reaction of the United States government is of course a factor that will vary somewhat according to current international and especially internal public opinion. A powerful internal sympathy for the Caribbean move would restrict the ability of the United States government to deal harshly with the nationalizing government. The most likely people in the United States to sympathize with Caribbean aspirations are the black people, but this will only be so if both they and the Caribbean governments see the move as part of the general movement for black liberation in Afro-America. This will involve the Caribbean people in support of the struggle of black America as well. The basis of this alliance will be the common experience of racial oppression in the plantation societies of the New World. But the bauxite-aluminum complex is involved in this struggle not only at the Caribbean end, but also by the fact that many of the plants of the aluminum companies are located in the racist economy of the American South, where they process Caribbean raw material. This provides another linkage between the black movements in the Caribbean and the United States.

The next step is to decide how far the cooperation of the companies is judged necessary for the success of the nationalization. This depends on how far it is thought desirable for the companies to continue to participate in the industry after nationalization in such forms as suppliers or customers and managers or marketers of the nationalized concerns. If a high premium is placed on this, then the nationalization strategy must include elements which make it attractive for the

166

companies to stay on in this position. Such elements are likely to be minority company ownership, compensation arrangements which are extremely or moderately generous, and continued close association in the areas of management, decision-making, and marketing. The Zambian and Chilean take-overs were very much like this, as we have seen. For purposes of clarity it might be better to call such arrangements by the name of Partial Nationalization (PN). The term, Full Nationalization (FN), will be used to describe take-overs where 100 percent share-ownership is acquired and the government also takes over management and marketing immediately.

The main advantage of PN compared to FN is that it usually ensures the uninterrupted flow of production and shipments in the industry. Thus where a high premium is placed on the uninterrupted maintenance of the tax revenue, foreign exchange and employment generated by the industry, PN is very attractive to the government. Since the FN alternative almost certainly involves some dislocation and disruption of revenue, foreign exchange and employment, it frightens a government which is not prepared for the various difficulties involved in this. As against this, there are the disadvantages of PN compared to FN. It involves continued company participation in basic decision-making, and continued direct company influence over expansion and processing policy. The companies usually bargain for tax and other concessions as their price for continued participation, so that in some cases—Zambia and the Chileanization of Kennecot—the profits they take out of the country remain the same or actually increase. The corollary is that in these cases the government's income as a result of PN remains the same or goes down—with the added twist that it is paying for its share participation, whereas before it got its income in the form of taxes. Hence in terms of *control* and in terms of *revenue*, PN can have its disadvantages. It depends to a large degree on the particular terms negotiated.

By contrast the FN option establishes immediate total control over profits, decision-making and marketing. The only reason that a government might not opt for FN is because of the judged difficulties in terms of production and marketing. The choice between FN and PN will therefore depend on the particular government, the particular industry, and the particular circumstances of the take-over. This will determine how far the government can rely on internal popular support, whether the technology necessary for production and expansion is monopolized by the parent firm or can be mobilized from other sources, how far new or different markets can be found, and what are the degree and nature of external opposition.

Two further points should be mentioned which usually escape the consideration of people or governments afraid of FN. First is the fact that the very dislocation and disruption caused by FN should be looked upon as part of the learning process, it is these difficulties which can stimulate the internal effort necessary to run the industry successfully. Ultimately the only way of learning is by trial and error in the process of actually *doing* the management and marketing. Secondly, one should bear in mind that since FN transfers the bulk of profits in the industry to the government and to the nation, the amount of revenue and foreign exchange generated *per ton* of exports will go up substantially. Thus we can afford to have a substantial contraction in the *total* tonnage of exports in the short run without a contraction in the net foreign exchange and revenues received before FN. The maintenance of employment in the short run could be a problem, but not necessarily so. This fact—that the *share* of the country in the total value of exports will rise so that a fall in the *total* export value could take place without reducing the country's *actual* receipts compared to the situation before FN—does give the nationalizing government some maneuverability which it is not always aware of before its basic policy decisions are made.

The above might be summed up by suggesting that the only instances in which will be clearly preferable to FN are when (1) the parent company of the firm to be taken over has an absolute, worldwide monopoly over the technology of production and over marketing, so that its cooperation is absolutely essential for the maintenance of production and shipments, or (2) when political circumstances are such that the government can rely only to a limited extent on domestic support during the period of dislocation and difficulties which may be caused by FN. The first does not apply to Guyana, Surinam, Jamaica, but the second can, under certain circumstances.

III. Conclusion

The purpose of this piece was to demonstrate why the

Caribbean bauxite industry needs to be nationalized and how it can be done. On both the first and second questions there is a great deal of confusion. Many people confuse the need to nationalize bauxite with the need to secure more income from the industry and to process the bauxite into aluminum and its products within the Caribbean. This is indeed part of the reason for nationalization, but the need goes much deeper than that. The basic reason for nationalization is to establish the precondition for the industry to be put to the service of the material development of the Caribbean people. When they are in a position of control, then their engineers, chemists, geologists, economists and other human resources will find myriad ways of doing this.

Many people, too, shrink from nationalization because of an instinctive fear of the responsibility which it would confer or because of its association with communism, or because of the spectre of United States Marines. Others are instinctively in favor, but are uncertain of proposing it because of a genuine lack of information as to how the industry works and how nationalization could be effected. This paper should, at least in part, pull away the veil of mystery, uncertainty and ignorance which has so far shrouded the issues.

FOOTNOTES

1. John Brown and Martin Butler, *The Production, Marketing and Consumption of Copper and Aluminum,* New York, Praeger, p. 52.
2. Cited in Paul Lemonin, "Nationalization and Management in Zambia," *New World Quarterly,* Mona, Jamaica, Vol. 5, No. 3.

BIBLIOGRAPHY

Brown, John, and Martin Butler, *The Production, Marketing and Consumption of Cooper and Aluminum,* New York, Praeger.

Girvan, Norman, *The Caribbean Bauxite Industry,* Institute of Social and Economic Research, University of the West Indies, Jamaica, 1967.

_____ "Multinational Corporations and Dependent Underdevelopment in Mineral Export Economics," Social and Economic Studies, Institute of Social and Economic Research, University of the West Indies, Jamaica. December. 1970

_____ The Denationalization of Caribbean Bauxite Alcoa in Guyana," *New World Quarterly,"* Mona, Jamaica, Vol. 5 No. 3, 1971.

Hoskins, Terence, "How to Counter Expropriation," Harvard Business Review.

Huggins, H.D. *Aluminum in Changing Communities,* London. Andre Deutsch in association with the Institute of Social and Economic Research, 1965.

Semonin, Paul, "Nationalization and Management in Zambia," *New World Quarterly,* Mona, Jamaica, Vol. 5, No. 3.

STUDIES IN FOREIGN INVESTMENT IN THE COMMONWEALTH CARIBBEAN
No.1 TRINIDAD AND TOBAGO
PART 1: THEORETICAL ANALYSIS

By

A. Mc Intyre

AND

B. Watson

Chapter 1

DIRECT FOREIGN INVESTMENT

Direct foreign investment is today by far the most important vehicle for long term private foreign investment. Unlike portfolio investment it is not merely a capital movement across national boundaries, but involves control of the enterprise. It is the potential for exercising extensive decision making powers which makes direct foreign investment a controversial topic.

Control may or may not be exercised in a manner which is contrary to the interest of the recipient country. Nevertheless, the factor of non-

STUDIES IN FOREIGN INVESTMENT IN THE COMMON-
WEALTH CARIBBEAN--NO. 1: TRINIDAD AND TOBAGO
(A Working Paper Published by the Institute
of Social and Economic Research, University
of the West Indies, Jamaica), June 1970,
pp. 1-16.

resident control underlines the possibility that the non-resident's view-point may not be coincident with the national interest. Whenever such divergencies occur costs are involved. Operation of the enterprise in the national interest demands that these areas of conflict be minimized.

Types of Direct Investment

Much of the discussion on the costs and benefits of direct investment centers on the multi-national corporation (MNC). Admittedly this is today the predominant form of foreign investment. But foreign investment may be associated with other forms. Some of these types have been important in the past history of the Caribbean and may be significant in some sectors of these economies today. The issues are different, and we therefore treat each separately.

Type I – 'Settler-Type' Investment[1] What is here called 'settler-type' investment refers to a situation where the investor, along with his capital moves to the territory, and the enterprise is not linked by owner-ship ties to a non-resident firm. There is the possibility of 'localization' as the investor or his heirs decide to settle permanently and the project becomes integrated into the local sector. This process of localization occurs quite frequently among well-defined immigrant groups. But it does not always occur. Residence may only be temporary until the business is well established.

This type of operation is unlikely to be a very large scale venture. It may be large in comparison to the average local firm, but is likely to be small in comparison with other resident foreign firms. It could be significant in activities such as tourism and professional services. In many of these areas nationals might not lack the expertise to run the industry. Nor, is there necessarily insufficient local capital to undertake the venture. Foreign investors might merely have been more willing to take the risks.

As was the case with the planters of the past, these investors are likely to have a short-run view and place a premium on very high profits. Consumption out of profits may be very high, but even when this is not so, the attachment to life in an overseas metropolitan center leads to the investment of profits in foreign securities. The growth effects on the local economy tend to be limited.

Type II – 'Putting Out' Investment. This differs from 'settler-type' investment since ownership and control resides abroad. There are, however, no links (through ownership) with a multinational corporation. Foreign owners arrange the day to day operations of the enterprise through hired management, but maintain overall direction in the alloca-tion of resources and the growth of its enterprises, individually and col-lectively.

The foreign owners may undertake to distribute the product on the

[1]This term and the one used to described Type II were suggested by Professor Terence Hopkins.

171

world market. In doing so sales are internalized. All 'sales' of the local firm are made to the agent; who in turn sells the product on the world markets. 'Prices' recorded for transactions with the agent can be quite arbitrary, and may be selected to depress the level of profits shown on local operations.

Type III — The Multinational Corporation. In the past direct investment has taken the forms outlined above. Today, it is largely channelled through the multinational corporation (an extension of the corporation into foreign countries). Activities of multinational corporations are well established in the West Indies - the Tate & Lyle operations in the sugar industry, the petroleum and bauxite companies, the international hotel chains, Woolworths and the petroleum companies in distribution, the Bookers operations in the Caribbean, and the almost complete domination of commercial banking by British, Canadian and United States branch banks. This is by no means a complete list, but illustrates some of the past developments. Moreover, the regional common market that is expected to evolve from the CARIFTA agreement, is likely to be an attraction for further foreign investment of this type.

Merger movements of past decades led to the emergence of the large firm in the United States of America and in other industrial countries. Today, industrial production is increasingly moving towards a pattern which makes the large corporation a necessary form of organization. U.S. Corporations have been leaders in this development, and firms in other industrialized countries have been led into mergers in order to effectively compete with the U.S. giants. Competition is increasingly on an international scale, and for various reasons many corporations have been led to expand their production abroad.

Whilst the corporation is a necessity in some activities, it is by no means an inevitable development in every type of business. A key factor has been the overriding importance of technology in modern industrial production.[2] Large scale organization has led to the corporation's control over technology. At the same time technology has emerged as a major factor in perpetuating the corporation as a form of business organization.

Technological leadership is now the decisive factor in maintaining a corporation's lead over its competitors. It is also the single most important factor which separates developed from underdeveloped countries.

To maintain this lead the corporation channels resources into research and development. It is driven to continually refine and improve its products, to develop and create markets for new products, and to seek new cost-reducing processes. This involves heavy expenditures. As technology becomes increasingly more complex, the expenditure on equipment increases, and there is need to employ very highly skilled personnel of all types. Decisions have to be taken well in advance of pro-

---

[2]Technology used in its widest sense- to cover not only productive processess, but also organizational and marketing techniques.

duction. The large corporation is in a much better position to organize the requisite skills and capital, and can more readily ensure that the demand will be created.

As the corporation grows it may extend its operations across national boundaries. At present it is the predominant private institution in the flow of capital and goods across national boundaries. By far the greatest proportion of private long term capital movements is transmitted via the MNC, and a significant proportion of international trade is accounted for by the movement of goods between divisions of multinational corporations.

There are a number of reasons why the corporation becomes international, and a few of these will be discussed. It is frequently asserted that international investment is attracted by the opportunity to earn higher profits than is possible in the home country. Studies have revealed that higher profits are often earned on foreign investment, but it seems certain that this is not a sufficient condition to induce overseas direct investment. In some types of industries other factors may carry much more weight with the investor.

Mining industries where world production is controlled by a handful of large companies, present an outstanding example. These corporations are usually integrated through all operations, from mining to the production of highly finished goods. Integration by-passes the market to reduce the risk and uncertainty which purchases of ore from independent producers would involve. The same principle is at work in their international operations. When new ore deposits are found abroad, investment is attracted by the need to control these deposits. The corporation may need additional reserves in order to expand its production. Alternatively, it may be driven to seek control of the new source rather than allow it to come under the control of competitors.

Under these circumstances, the MNC will follow new resource discoveries; but the extent of its operations, and therefore the impact on the receiving country, are dependent on other considerations. Where extensive advantages are to be gained by locating processing facilities near to the source of supply, the investment is more extensive, and the benefits to the receiving country more substantial.

It is doubtful just how significant these locational advantages can be. For many years Caribbean bauxite has been shipped to the United States of America in crude form, and Jamaican bauxite is now being processed as far away as Ghana. Trinidad on the other hand processes crude oil imported from the Middle East and Africa.

In the case of other resource based industries (tourism and agriculture are the two of significance in the Commonwealth Caribbean) the picture is similar. Investment is induced by the presence of an essential factor of production not readily available elsewhere - climate and soil types in agriculture, beaches and sunshine in tourism.

Growth of the large corporation has come at a time when decolonization has given rise to a number of nation states each pursuing policies aimed at establishing and maintaining economic independence. Two conflicting tendencies are at work. The corporation sees its progress in terms of its share of world markets. Nation states are interested in promoting industrial development, and to this end are prepared to use control instruments such as tariffs and import restrictions. The corporation is disturbed by the possibility of exporting to a market in competition with rivals protected by tariffs and import restrictions. In such circumstances it is driven to produce abroad. Only in this way can it defend its overseas markets.

This seems to have been an important factor in the spread of the multinational corporation to countries as different as Canada and India. The Watkins Report[3] cites this as the major factor in motivating foreign investment in secondary manufacturing industry. Kidron[4] notes that foreign management often sees this as the most compelling reason for direct overseas investment, while profitability is hardly mentioned. He notes also that every tightening of import controls in India since the 1957-1958 exchange crisis has been followed by a rush of foreign applications for industrial licences, capital issue permits, etc.[5]

Commerce, Banking, Construction, and Services, are some types of activity where exports cannot be an alternative to direct investment. Profitability of the enterprise is likely to play a more important role in attracting direct investment in these spheres.

As the corporation evolved, the centre of control has shifted from shareholders to the management team.[6] Accompanying this shift in control is a change in objectives. The corporation is still concerned with profitability, but it now operates with a longer horizon. Growth of the corporation has now become a major objective and organization is geared to this end. When it expands abroad the subsidiary becomes a mere division within the world-wide corporation, and its operations are determined in accordance with the overall objectives of the MNC. The profitability and growth of local operations become subordinate to the profitability and growth of the MNC taken as a whole. It is to be emphasised that the interests of the MNC may not necessarily be inconsistent with the growth and development of the resident branch. Nevertheless, the possibility of a divergence of interest does exist, for the MNC has several alternatives open to it. Integration of world production may replace the development of comprehensive production facilities in the domestic economy. (It may also prevent the growth of local business when a possibly large purchaser is restricted to importing from associates rather than buy from non-affiliates). The expansion of a subsidiary in one country may take place at the expense of expansion elsewhere.

One area of conflict has been the pricing of non-market transactions. As the corporation grew in its home territory, vertical integration re-

[3]*Foreign Ownership and the Structure of Canadian Industry*, Report of the Task Force on the Structure of Canadian Industry, Queen's Printer, Ottawa, 1968.

[4]M. Kidron, *Foreign Investments in India*, Oxford University Press, 1965.

[5]*Ibid.*, p. 254.

[6]See J.K. Galbraith. *The New Industrial State* for a description of this change.

174

placed market transactions with purely internal transfers. International expansion has carried this development into world trade. A significant proportion of international trade today is merely a movement of goods between divisions of multinational corporations. 'Prices' recorded on these transactions are arbitrary valuations determined by the MNC. The receiving country wants 'prices' set so as to record the highest possible profits on local operations. The MNC may or may not pursue such a policy. It's objective will be to select prices to maximize world-wide profits after tax, bearing in mind the varying rates of taxation in its home country, the receiving country, and any other countries involved in the various transactions.

A great deal has been written about the problems of pricing, and governments in the Caribbean have, in the past, had to deal with this situation. In mining especially, problems have arisen, and significant increases in the tax share have been made by negotiating new pricing agreements.

Another possible area of conflict crops up in relation to the location of production facilities for the further processing of raw materials, or for the production of the necessary inputs. Decisions are taken by the MNC in relation to its world operations. For one reason or another the decision may be taken to expand existing plants or to set up new productive facilities elsewhere. From the viewpoint of the developing country, maximum local production is desirable wherever the volume of output makes it a feasible alternative to imports or exports.

Marketing restrictions on subsidiaries are also likely to create disagreements. Where a subsidiary produces the products of its parent under the same brand names, it is often allocated a specific market area. In some cases, it may be limited to the territory in which it is located. In others a regional market is defined. In any case limits are placed on the growth and development of the local subsidiary.

One final area of clashing interest must be mentioned. The corporation's growth and development is, in many cases, tied to its ability to develop and market new products, to develop more economical methods of processing, and new uses for raw materials. Much of the expenditure on research and development is centered in the home country of the MNC, and is biased towards the market conditions and raw materials available there. Some developments may have a favourable impact on the local subsidiary, as is the case when new uses for a product increase the demand for the raw material. In some cases the effects may be unfavourable. Improvements in processing may reduce the quantity of raw material required per unit of output; or the development of substitutes based on raw materials more readily available in the home country, may eventually lead to the subsidiary's demise.

It is inherent in the MNC that such divergences of interest will occur. A particular country may be getting more or less than its share of development through the MNC. Nevertheless, the fact that interests may diverge points to the need for periodical assessment of the benefits and costs to the economy, and for policy measures to ensure that benefits are maximized.

Chapter 2

COSTS AND BENEFITS OF DIRECT INVESTMENT

In the paragraphs above an outline was given of the different forms which direct investment may take, with a sketch of the behavioral patterns associated with each. This has a bearing on any assessment of the costs and benefits of direct investment, since the costs and benefits to a developing country concerned with rapid economic growth and development, depend on the outlook and behaviour of direct investment enterprises operating in the economy.

Direct investment has been described as a 'package deal' bringing not merely capital, but also products, entrepreneurship, markets, and technology to the receiving country. The various components of the package carry different weights depending both on the type of direct investment, and on the activity in which direct investment is made. The costs and benefits vary widely with the components of the package brought by particular enterprises. Investment by multinational corporations in mining and manufacturing probably makes the most substantial contributions in terms of the 'package'.

Costs and benefits are not static. What may be an immediate benefit may involve heavy costs in the future and visa versa. In what follows an attempt is made to show both the immediate and long term implications of direct investment. Costs and benefits are discussed under various headings, viewed from the standpoint of what developing countries such as those of the Commonwealth Caribbean want from direct investment. It assumes that economic growth which relies entirely on entrepreneurial initiative and technological developments from abroad, can never be accepted as true development. Indeed, the capacity for growth under such circumstances is severely limited by the paucity of natural resources which are still the most important inducement to foreign investment in underdeveloped countries today.

SAVINGS AND INVESTMENT

Foreign investment is often justified by the argument that underdeveloped countries are short of savings and this is one way of increasing the pool of savings available to the economy. Current national accounting practice tends to over-estimate the real contribution of foreign savings to local investment. Appendix I discusses this problem.

Ignoring the difficulties associated with measuring the contribution of foreign savings, an act of direct investment can be said to channel foreign savings into specific productive activities in the local economy. What the underdeveloped country wants is an expansion of productive facilities in a way which does not stifle local entrepreneurs. Therefore,

176

foreign investment which merely takes over local businesses already in operation is less desirable than investment which brings in new productive assets.[7] This is especially so when takeovers are not accompanied by any significant changes which would improve the performance of the industry. This disadvantage would be reduced in so far as the former owners of the assets re-invested their receipts in the economy. All too often, however, receipts are consumed or invested in foreign securities.

Direct investment which adds to the productive capacity of the economy may itself have an adverse effect on the investment carried out by local businesses. This is likely to be important in sectors where local business firms are well established, and investment opportunities are limited. For example, this could well occur in sectors such as Distribution.

Domestic investment may also be deterred by the heightened competition for scarce complementary factors which the investment may create. Local firms and prospective local entrepreneurs may not be able to compete successfully with resident foreign enterprises which have the backing of a larger parent firm.

The net effect of foreign investment is, therefore, likely to be somewhat less than is indicated by the dollar value of the investment. The negative effect on local investment is not merely the sum total of investment foregone. Foreign investment is likely to have a higher capital/output ratio than the local investment which it replaces and, therefore, something more than a dollar's worth of foreign investment is required to compensate for each dollar of local investment foregone.

While foreign investment may reduce local investment, it can also stimulate investment by increasing the opportunities open to the local sector. The potential for such growth is likely to be significant only when the enterprise is large, and even then the local firm may not benefit. For example, the demand for construction services is large only in the initial phases of the project. Demand for inputs when large enough to warrant local production, may nevertheless be filled by associates resident elsewhere, or produced by the firm itself.[8]

Although foreign investment gives the country access to a new source of saving, an extensive foreign sector goes a long way toward reinforcing the dependence on foreign savings. The handful of large corporations which are the driving force in industrial economies, play a major role in generating savings and converting them into productive investment. Reinvested profits become a major source of investment funds, and they contribute to the corporation's ability to grow. When, however, large and profitable areas of the economy are foreign controlled, the direction of a significant proportion of profit income may be in the hands of nonresidents. A high proportion of this income may be reinvested. But the

---

[7]'New' in the sense of not previously operating in the territory.

[8]This includes also the case where resident foreign firms benefit at the expense of the local sector.

investor has the choice of allocating his savings between his local operations and his enterprises elsewhere. To the extent that the decision is favourable to the domestic economy, expansion takes place. At the same time, this expansion expresses itself as a new flow of foreign investment, which continues to reinforce the existing dependent situation.[9]

Other potential sources of saving may be enhanced by direct investment. When a mineral resource is being exploited by foreign investment, government's share of value added could be quite large. However, if Government assumes a very limited role in the business sector, it cannot break the continued dependence on foreign investment that is inherent in an extensive foreign sector.

FOREIGN EXCHANGE

Under ideal conditions, investment funds used to set up a direct investment enterprise in the receiving country, should not draw upon the scarce foreign exchange reserves of underdeveloped countries. Any tendency to borrow capital locally reduces the initial foreign exchange contribution, and may even draw on the scarce foreign exchange reserves of the country, when amounts borrowed exceed the purely local content of the investment. There is a real possibility that this could happen in the Commonwealth Caribbean, where sterling area companies are allowed free access to local financial markets.

In addition to the initial contribution, the firm's operations set up new charges on the foreign exchange receipts of the country. Investment income, royalties and management fees, other service charges, and payments for imported inputs, are some of the major outflows likely to result from current operations. To this must be added any consumer imports resulting from additional income generated by the investment. The net effect on the balance of payments therefore, depends on the value of additional exports or import substitutes produced by the enterprise.[10] Where overseas receipts (actual receipts or reduced outflows) are small, the effect on the balance of payments may be unfavourable. Public Utilities, Construction, and Services, are some areas where foreign investment tends to be a drain on foreign exchange reserves.[11]

Streeten[12] argues for the separation of these overall effects into two components. The first focuses attention on inflows and outflows associated with the investment as *foreign* investment. Direct investment involves,

[9]See below for Trinidad (Chap. V). About 60% of profit income earned by resident enterprises accrues to non-residents (and this makes no allowance for the probable understatement of profits by the companies).

[10]No allowance has been made for the foreign exchange contributions of production displaced by the investment on the assumption that they are likely to be small. In any particular case where they are significant these must be included in an assessment of the costs and benefits under this heading.

[11]Not including tourist services.

[12]P. Streeten, "The Role of Foreign Private Investment in the Development Process", Venture Vol. 22, No. 1.

as he puts it, the flow of money across the exchanges for the construction of the project, and the subsequent repatriation of profits, and perhaps capital. These then, are the distinguishing foreign exchange effects of direct investment.

The second component consists of the inflows and outflows created by the operation of the enterprises; because, as Streeten argues, these are inherent in the nature of the investment, whether foreign or local. There is some merit in this approach. The "foreign exchange effects" (Streeten's definition) are invariably negative in the long run, and separating the two focuses attention on the fact that alternatives[13] involves lower costs (or alternatively increases the benefits) in terms of contributions to the foreign exchange reserves. There is, however, an objection to this analysis. The operations of multinational corporations may involve foreign exchange costs and benefits quite different from those attributable to a local enterprise or even perhaps a joint venture. Subsidiaries manufacturing the products of the parent corporation and using the same brand names, are usually allocated a share of the multinational corporation's world market. Early growth of the enterprise may, therefore, be greater than it would have been without a ready-made market. In the long run, however, circumscribed markets could limit the growth of exports and so reverse the effect on the balance of payments.

Another example centres on the reliance on imported inputs, which from the point of view of the multinational corporation may be the most efficient way of organizing its world operations. Inputs may be imported even when the volume of production makes it feasible to develop local sources of raw materials, or to set up plants for the domestic production of inputs. The drain on foreign exchange receipts would, therefore, be greater than might occur with local development of the industry.

By far the most important difference is created by the multinational corporation's ability to undervalue exports and overvalue imported inputs in 'trade' with associates. Articles which are transferred between divisions of multinational corporations are seldom traded on world markets, and valuations cannot be checked. When they can be checked, special discounts on these sales and other charges, are used to vary prices. It is conceivable that sales and inputs may be valued to the advantage of the resident subsidiary. Since, however, all available evidence suggests an opposite tendency, it is assumed here, that foreign direct investment imposes additional costs in terms of foreign exchange receipts and payments.

TECHNOLOGY

Technology, used here to mean both productive techniques and know-how in administration, marketing and other business techniques, has

---

[13]For example local ownership or any combination of foreign and local ownership.

been held to be one of the most important, if not the most important contribution of direct investment. Direct investment brings with it access to the technology of the parent company.

Direct investment is by no means the only avenue by which a country may have access to technology. It may try to develop its own - a long and costly process; or purchase it through licensing agreements, management contracts, or by participating in joint ventures with overseas firms. Some productive processes are fairly standard and readily available, and the costs involved in developing local expertise in running such industries need not be forbiddingly high. It could well prove more economical to pursue this course, rather than to rely on foreign investment in some of these activities.

In other cases, firms maintain strict control of processes which they have developed, and may refuse to pass on this knowledge to firms over which they have no control. Transfer is likely to be freer when the local firm is a subsidiary; and the establishment of the industry might, therefore, not be possible without direct investment. This may justify direct investment when rejected on other grounds.

While, however, the resident firm may have free access to the technological know-how of the parent, this is by no means the full contribution which the underdeveloped country expects. Ideally what is required is a transfer of technology in such a way that it becomes available to local producers (actual or potential), and leads to a process of self-sustaining growth in technology. This may be at variance with the interests of the MNC, whose advantage may rest with its technological expertise. A real transfer may not, therefore, take place. But it must be done. Continued technological dependence can never lead to the healthy growth of local business. The history of the Commonwealth Caribbean is instructive. These territories have been accustomed to 'modern' production and organizational methods for centuries, and are yet technologically backward.

The failure to transmit technological dynamism may stem from several factors, some inherent in direct investment itself. In the first place, the provision of management and technicians by the investor restricts the know-how transferred to the nationals of the host country. The ease with which the multinational corporation can make such personnel available is sometimes cited as an advantage of such investment. Whilst this may be very beneficial in the early stages of development, it can, however, restrict the development of local expertise, and thereby the means by which know-how is transferred to the local sector.[14]

Of even more importance is the possibility that crucial areas of expertise may be centered abroad. In particular, the control of research and development tends to be centered in the metropolitan countries, and this is a key area in promoting technological dynamism. Almost equally

---

[14]Trinidad provides an interesting example. After decades of experience in the Petroleum Industry the National Petroleum company is forced into a joint venture with an American firm in order to get the expertise required to run the former B.P. holdings.

important is the know-how required in marketing products abroad. Subsidiaries producing brands of parent companies are often allocated markets already developed by the sales organization of the MNC. It is the transfer of such expertise which will make underdeveloped countries technologically dynamic; and policy should, therefore, aim at maximizing such contributions. It is particularly important if the Commonwealth Caribbean hopes to develop a significant export trade in manufactured goods.

ENTREPRENEURSHIP

In the 'package' of productive factors brought by direct investment, entrepreneurship plays a most important role. It has sometimes been argued that this is the single most important factor in stimulating development. Where the supply of entrepreneurship is abundant other problems become soluble. Savings will be mobilized for investment, and markets will be developed.

These arguments are to a certain extent valid. Whilst technology has become increasingly important in industrial production, and its control by the large corporations makes it impossible to rule out direct investment (or some form of collaboration), there are still potential areas for development where technology is unimportant (e.g. Tourism), or can be obtained through licensing agreements or joint ventures. Local entrepreneurship can seek out and develop these activities; and where the long-run interests of the entrepreneur are dependent on technological dynamism, local enterprises can be geared to achieving this end.

Direct investment brings entrepreneurship, and so fills an existing gap. But it makes a more substantial contribution when it stimulates the growth of local entrepreneurship. Similarly, if direct investment has the effect of stunting the development of indigenous entrepreneurship, it imposes severe costs on the economy.

Direct investment may stimulate local entrepreneurship by providing a market for outputs, thereby increasing the range of investment opportunities. Investment and additional income to residents create demands for locally produced goods and services. The strength of these effects depends on the size of the project and the policies of investors. Small investments transmit little demand.

As has already been observed, demand for construction services may be substantial.[15] Demand for inputs may be restricted by imports from overseas associates or by the setting up of comprehensive operations, exploiting all major linkages within the enterprise. There is also a tendency for foreign firms to bring in other overseas firms for providing auxiliary services.

Transmission effects are also likely to be limited in other ways. The investor tends to deal with established rather than new firms. To the extent, therefore, that foreign firms already dominate sectors such

[15]Especially in tourism; and in Jamaica and Guyana-Bauxite.

as construction, manufacturing of building materials, packaging etc., then new foreign investment might not have much impact.[16]

The techniques of production, management and organization of the foreign investor may improve the performance of local firms, but this depends on the strength of the local sector. Foreign investment could drive a local entrepreneur out of business, before he has had a chance to develop sufficient expertise to be able to withstand competition from the foreign investor.

Free entry on the part of foreign firms may deter local entrepreneurs. In manufacturing, the multinational corporation brings its own brands with assured local and perhaps regional markets. As part of a world wide group of companies the resident branch cannot be compared with small local firms. Local entrepreneurs may, therefore, be deterred by the possibility that a multinational firm may use these advantages to drive them out of business. This is a real possibility. G. Arthur Brown has cited the case of a Jamaican paint manufacturer who was literally forced to sell his business to a multinational corporation.[17] Competition initiated by the overseas firm with a well established local market, drove the manufacturer out of business. Local production continued, since the MNC subsequently bought out the local company's assets.

Although protection from imports can prevent an exact repetition of this case, it does not rule out the possibility that the MNC will set up production locally, and use its superior advantages to the detriment of the local entrepreneur. And when the multinational corporation is already producing locally, the threat is similar to the example cited. It could clearly deter local entrepreneurship. What effect this has is, however, a matter of conjecture. Certainly, the tendency of local entrepreneurs to replicate foreign products as opposed to the development of indigenous products, indicates that these considerations may be stunting the growth of local entrepreneurship. Moreover, the long history of direct foreign investment in the Caribbean has not given much stimulation to local entrepreneurship. This is true also of other economies where foreign ownership is extensive.

SKILLS

Any extension of the productive base in the economy will contribute to the pool of skilled labour, though a take-over might contribute nothing in this direction. Skilled labour is used here in its widest sense. Even the mere introduction of a greater number of workers to the discipline of industrial and business habits, is a contribution to the climate within

---

[16]Local firms in Jamaica have been complaining about this in relation to the construction of the Alpart project.

[17]"Economic Development and the Private Sector" *Social and Economic Studies*, Vol. 7, No. 3, p. 113.

which development thrives. At the opposite end of the scale are managerial skills.

Some skills may be less readily passed on to nationals. In particular, foreign managers readily available within the multinational corporation, may be used for running the enterprise instead of training local managers. When managerial skills are passed on to nationals, these managers may become inaccessible to local firms. The flow of such personnel from foreign to local firms appears to be quite small, perhaps because the larger size of the firm, accentuated by its international character, offers wider career opportunities. As nationals move higher in the managerial heirachy they tend to become part of the international management team. They may even be transferred overseas, thereby contributing to the 'brain drain'.

Training costs are not all borne by the foreign investor. New entrants tend to bid away skilled labour from local firms and the public sector, especially the latter.

EMPLOYMENT

Governments in the region are often concerned with the employment created by various projects. This is a frequently used statistic in annual economic surveys. No doubt this aspect of foreign investment is one to which they attach great importance.

The net impact on employment depends on the effect of the investment on the operations of other resident enterprises, local or foreign. Indirect effects are negative when the new investment deters other investments, and positive in so far as the investment and its operation generate demand from resident enterprises. In general, the net result is likely to be a gain, especially when operations are large.

It should, however, be pointed out that the gain is due to the investment, and would be available under alternative patterns of ownership. Local ownership may even increase the labour content, to the extent that it establishes greater linkages within the economy. Moreover, the foreign investor may be biased toward more capital-intensive techniques. Not only is capital not a scarce factor to the foreign investor, but he might also want to minimize his contact with an alien labour force.

COMPETITION

When local firms are well established in a particular activity, the competition offered by new enterprises may improve the performance of the local sector. The entry of Woolworths and Hi-Lo into retail trade in Jamaica, are possible instances where foreign investment made a considerable impact on the performance of local firms. However, this contribution tends to be a gain only when local firms are well established. Competition which drives local firms out of business may not be a gain. It may be used as a weapon to remove rivals from the market.[18]

[18]See above p. 13.

Competition in this sense is a monopolistic practice, for the local firm is at a disadvantage when faced with the usually larger resident foreign enterprise backed by the resources of a world-wide group of companies. It would be almost impossible for local firms with little experience in an industry, to successfully resist such competition.

Foreign investors are themselves wary of any "unequal" competition. They are driven to produce behind tariff barriers because, as they argue, competition from outside with rivals producing inside would be "unequal".[19] In the same way the local firm needs protection from the "unequal" competition which the resident subsidiary may offer.

PUBLIC REVENUES

Direct investment enterprises may contribute to government revenues, but contributions are likely to be significant only in the long run. Mining is perhaps an exception. Foreign investment which exploits a mineral resource, tends to make significant contributions even in the short-run. On the other hand, countries which insist on a share in the equity of these industries have significantly improved their receipts.

Incentive legislation that aims at attracting foreign investment, not only reduces taxable income, but may have an adverse effect on government's ability to tax business. Not only is there a tendency for incentives to be given to all new manufacturers, whether this is justified or not, but demands for an extension of these subsidies to other areas of the economy can hardly be avoided.

It is not this, however, which has made the tax-take from direct investment enterprises a controversial issue. It is rather the fact that integrated world operations, and contacts with wholly owned selling agents abroad, allow room for tax avoidance.[20] The issue is most keenly felt when the enterprise is a major tax contributor, and when the tax-take is one of the major local shares in the output of the industry.

Vertically integrated multinational corporations have perhaps the greatest leverage for arbitrary assignment of profits between countries. "Purchases" from and "sales" to affiliates permit arbitrary pricing. When operations cover shipping the scope is further widened. The tendency to register ships in tax havens makes an increase in transportation costs attractive. Other methods of tax avoidance involve the overvaluation of assets, (and therefore, a part of depreciation charges are really profits), and the transfer of profits in the form of royalties, technical and managerial charges, interest, and so on.

[19]Kidron, *op. cit.*, p. 225 "......... In conversation, foreign managements are invariably eloquent on the dangers of 'unequal competition', that is, competition from *outside* a tariff wall, with a known international rival, and normally see in such dangers the final and compelling reason for investment".

[20]Tourism provides a unique example of the latter where "Agents" are paid heavy commissions on bookings.

One can argue that whilst the scope exists, it may not necessarily be used to undervalue the share of local profits. The absence of any free markets for some of the products '"traded" between associates of multi-national corporations, makes it quite impossible to say just what is a fair share of local operations. It is very likely that the investor may wish to undervalue profits in order to minimize local pressures for re-investment of profits. Certainly what evidence there is, suggests that profits are often 'depressed on operations in underdeveloped countries. Kidron[21] cites the tea industry in India where products are consigned direct from producers in India to buyers in different parts of the world. Yet all 'sales' are recorded as made to the United Kingdom investors who in turn 'sell' at much higher prices to the buyers. Enquiries in other industries in India found that profits were consistently depressed. Here in the Caribbean, Girvan's study of the Bauxite Industry[22] has noted such widely different 'prices' that it gives cause for concern. The evidence seems to be that exports from Guyana to the United States of America have been undervalued, with profits attributed to the shipping operations.

NON-ECONOMIC COSTS

In the foregoing paragraphs, the discussion of the costs and benefits of direct investment have been confined to the conventional economic categories. However, there are important non-economic costs that flow from substantial dependence upon overseas capital and initiative. Among these are psychological attitudes that are developed within the community, which place a premium upon fate as opposed to rational planning as the main influence over social and economic change.

Since it comes to be believed that one cannot really fashion the course of economic events, considerable resources of time (and some-times of money) are devoted to wooing foreign governments and business-men - playing a 'court jester' role as it were. In its worst manifesta-tions, this leads to deferential postures that are not short of outright begging, and to a conviction that one can only prosper at the expense of one's neighbours. When communities get caught up in this state of mind, the achievement of self-sustaining growth and economic transformation become well-nigh impossible. And failure to make progress in these directions, encourages the view that change can only occur through radi-cal overthrow of the existing social and economic order. Foreign domi-nated economies tend, therefore, to become progressively explosive.

Although these psychological attitudes and their consequences might not be serious or widespread in the Commonwealth Caribbean at the present time, it is not inconceivable that they could grow in importance, under the continuing influence of laissez-faire policies toward the foreign investor.

[21]*Op. cit.*, p. 277.

[22]N. Girvan, *The Caribbean Bauxite Industry*, Institute of Social & Economic Research, U.W.I., Jamaica, 1967.

A Caribbean Social Type: Neither "Peasant" Nor "Proletarian"[1]

By

RICHARD FRUCHT

Studies and commentaries on Caribbean societies have made it clear that such concepts as "peasant" and "proletarian" are not categorical, but variable.[2] In this paper I attempt to show that what may also be of importance in understanding Caribbean societies besides the nature of the category ("peasant" or "proletarian") is the nature of the variable relationships characterizing the society. I want to show that particularly for the smaller islands, such as Nevis,[3] the people are categorically neither peasants nor proletarians. Rather the situation may be comprehended by making use of Marx's analytic distinction between the *means of production*, that is, the tools and techniques, *and relations of production*, that is, what we usually mean by the social division of labour as well as the articulation of the productive economy and the social organization, including property and power relations. More specifically, I want to show that during the period after slave emancipation in 1834 and until the end of the second World War, Nevisian society could be characterized as exhibiting a *peasant-like* means of production along with *proletarian-like* relations of production. The argument here rests on discriminating between kinds of sharecropping or *metayage* relationships.

Most of our discussions about peasantry and proletariat in the Caribbean have been based on work carried out in the Greater Antilles[4] — Jamaica, Haiti and Puerto Rico — and in some of the more important Lesser or Eastern Antilles[5] such as Martinique and Trinidad, as well as Guyana. At the risk

[1]The data on which this article is based were collected in 1961 and 1962-63 during fieldwork supported by Brandeis University and the Research Institute for the Study of Man. This article was read as a paper before the American Anthropological Association in Pittsburgh, 1966.

[2]See, for instance, Sidney Mintz, Foreword to *Sugar and Society in the Caribbean*, by R. Guerra y Sanchez. Yale University Press, New Haven, 1964, especially pages xxiv-xxxviii, also, A. Norton and G. Cumper, 'Peasant', 'Plantation' and 'Urban' Communities in Rural Jamaica: A Test of the Validity of the Classification, *Social and Economic Studies*, 15:4:338-352, 1966.

[3]Nevis is a unit of the former British Caribbean colony of St. Kitts-Nevis-Anguilla in the northern Lesser Antilles. It has an area of 36 square miles, and a population of approximately 13,000. Sugar-cane and Sea Island cotton were the major cash crops.

[4]A comprehensive bibliography of the British and formerly British Caribbean, edited by Lambros Comitas is forthcoming. Herewith are some references I have found useful. M. Horowitz, "A Typology of Rural Community Forms in the Caribbean," *Anthropological Quarterly* 33:4:177-187, 1960; S. Mintz, "Historical Sociology of the Jamaican Church-Founded Free Village System," *De West Indische Gids* 38:46-70, 1958; A. Metraux, *Making a Living in the Marbial Valley* (Haiti), UNESCO, 1951; J. Steward, (ed.), *The People of Puerto Rico*, University of Illinois Press, 1956.

[5]M. Horowitz, *Morne Paysan: Peasant Village in Martinique*, Holt, Rinehart and Winston, Inc., New York, 1967; M. Freilich, *Cultural Diversity Among Trinidadian Peasants*, Ph.D. Dissertation, Columbia University, 1960; R. Farley, "Rise of a Peasantry in British Guiana," *Social and Economic Studies* 2:4, 1954.

SOCIAL AND ECONOMIC STUDIES, 1967, Vol. 16, No. 3, pp. 295-300.

of over-simplifying, such peasantries are to be found in communities on lands marginal to the needs of the plantations, in the highlands and sometimes in the arid lowlands. A primary characteristic of peasantry is household production of subsistence crops on small plots, with cash crops produced according to location and market conditions.[6] Occasional involvement in wage labour on plantations in order to supplement cash needs is also a feature of Caribbean peasantries. They are usually contrasted with the part-societies of plantation labourers, the rural proletariat, who live on or near plantations and whose livelihood depends primarily upon the sale of their labour to the plantations and supplemented by desultory cultivation of subsistence crops on garden plots, when and if available.[7]

I want to point out that the word "peasant" is not to be here understood as a categorical concept describing a subculture or kind of community. It is not to be so understood because the so-called peasantry of Nevis has always been inextricably bound to the plantation system or to some other system of wage labour in more than an occasional sense. This is an artifact of geography, of economic history, and of the economic and political predominance of the industrial, colonial power.[8]

In essence I want to make what I hope is not a too simplified distinction: that in Nevis, whereas there is a peasant-like *means* of production, which includes cultivation of small plots with the use of household labour and traditional manual technology,[9] the *relations* of production are proletarian, that is, based on the sale of labour for wages either paid in cash or in kind, and the latter through systems of sharecropping, farming-out, and under conditions of male labour emigration. Finally, the existence together and in alternation of seemingly disparate *means* and *relations* of production is an adaptation to the vicissitudes of a marginal economy.

The development of a peasant-like means of production — household production — began after the emancipation of slaves in 1834, because of geographical and economic factors. In the first place, free villages of the type founded in Jamaica, for instance, did not develop in the Leeward Islands since there was no land available either for slaves or freedmen. All the land was alienated and under the control of the plantation-owners. The post-emancipation villages established on free-hold or lease-hold tenure grew on estate boundaries, along the sides of steep ravines, too steep for profitable sugar-cane cultivation, on the arid lowlands, and on the steep upper slopes of the central mountain masses. In short, the villages were founded on land

---

[6]Support for this emphasis on household production within the peasant type can be found in: Eric Wolf, *Peasants*, Prentice-Hall Englewood Cliffs, 1966, especially pages 13-15; Janet Fitchin, "Peasantry As A Social Type", in *Proceedings of the 1961 Annual Spring Meeting of the American Ethnological Society*, Seattle, 1961, especially page 115; Teodor Shanin, "The Peasantry as a Political Factor", *Sociological Review* 14:1:5-27, 1966, especially pages 6-10.

[7]Sidney Mintz, "The Folk-Urban Continuum and the Rural Proletarian Community", *American Journal of Sociology* 59:136-143, 1953; Eric Wolf and Sidney Mintz, "Haciendas and Plantations in Middle America and the Antilles", *Social and Economic Studies* 6:3:380-412, 1957.

[8]This theme is elaborated in R. Frucht, *Community and Context in a Colonial Society*, Ph.D. Dissertation, Brandeis University, 1966.

[9]Based on use of pitchfork and hoe, wielded equally well by men and women.

marginal to the plantations' uses, but on or near them so that they served, in effect, as dormitories for the labourers. Such villages are still found in St. Kitts and Antigua where plantations predominate. In Nevis, however, the plantation economy slowly became a small-holders' economy through the failings of the sugar — and, later, the cotton — markets. But the small-holders' economy in this island is not a peasant economy — that is, it is *not always* and has never been *only* a peasant economy.

To some extent, the economy based on household production of subsistence and cash crops on small plots was instituted in order to preserve a way of life based on the social relations of plantation production. In Nevis, for instance, the end of the apprenticeship period in 1838 and the final emancipation of slaves, together with the threatened position of the entire West Indian sugar industry led to a call for debt payments on the part of the factors and creditors of plantation operators. The resulting cash shortage and the necessity of maintaining plantation operations for the benefit of the planters and absentee-owners resident in England led to the adoption of forms of sharecropping as the means by which sugar-cane cultivation could be carried on. The hallmark of sharecropping is the use of household labour, but the share which remains with the labourer can be considered a form of wage payment — not in cash, but in kind. In other words, the freed slaves were forced to remain on plantation lands, and the lack of cash with which to pay these freedmen even low wages impelled the planters to pay their labourers in kind — through the means of what may be referred to as the share-wage.

The share-wage is one form of sharecropping. It refers to a situation in which the cropper, or labourer, supplies the tools — in this case hoe and pitch-fork — and the labour — his own and that of his household. The landowner, on the other hand, supplies the seed, the fertilizer, the insecticide, and supervision in the person of a "chargehand" or overseer. Furthermore, within this relationship it is the owner who decides which crop shall be cultivated. In this way the share which remains with the sharecropper or labourer can be considered a form of wages in kind.[10]

The other form of sharecropping is what I refer to as the share-rent, and is similar to the share-tenant relationship characteristic of the American south.[11] Under these conditions, the tenant supplies tools, seed, fertilizer, labour, etc., the landowner merely lets the use of his land. The decision as to what to cultivate remains with the tenant, and he may hire labourers to work his plot for him. The share given to the landowner, then, can be considered a form of rent in kind. In Nevis, the share-rent relationship was engaged in primarily and perhaps only by what I have previously referred to as Special People[12] — an upper lower class composed of millhands, carters,

10See C. Y. Shephard, *Peasant Agriculture in the Leeward and Windward Islands*, Imperial College of Tropical Agriculture, Trinidad, 1945, pp. 5-10.

11R. Vance, *Human Factors in Cotton Culture*, University of North Carolina Press, 1929, pp. 253-271..

12R. Frucht, "Remittances and the Economy in a Small West Indian Island", read before the American Anthropological Association, 1963.

overseers, mechanics and other skilled or semi-skilled individuals able to accumulate cash wages. The share-wage relationship was never engaged in by this type, but always by households of agricultural labourers.

The use of household labour on small plots for the benefit of the plantation was further reinforced during the middle of the nineteenth century in spite of conditions of available cash, because of new techniques of intensive cultivation of sugar cane introduced from Barbados. Under this farming-out system, sugar cane planting was carried out by gangs hired by the estate after which households were given one to two-acre plots to care for, for which they were paid a weekly wage. The cane cutting was done by gangs which invariably included men from the households who were given farms. This system gave the advantage of intensive care which produced greater yields and was even more eminently suited to the cultivation of cotton, a more delicate crop, which was introduced at the beginning of this century. But the farming-out system was common on the few large, well-capitalized estates, while the many smaller estates still relied on sharecropping.

Finally, another factor in the instituting of peasant-like adaptations or household production is the emigration of male labourers which began during the depression of the 1880's and which continued to the end of the first quarter of this century. During the eighties and nineties there was emigration to the gold fields of Venezuela, and to other islands in search of employment. According to the 1891 census there were 83 males for every 100 females in Nevis. After the turn of the century, opportunities for overseas male employment increased. In 1911 there were 74 males for every 100 females in Nevis, and in 1921, 68 males per 100 females. Female predominance under sharecropping and farming-out worked as well if not better with cotton, which was introduced in 1904. Demands of cotton cultivation are not as great as those of sugar cane. Weeding and picking cotton was primarily the work of women, children and elderly men; a division of labour which exists to this day. In a real sense, during the early part of this century women engaged in peasant-like means of production, although both they and the emigrant male labourers were engaged in proletarian *relations* of production: wage labour, either for cash or for kind.

The co-existence of peasant means of production and proletarian relations of production continued until the end of the second World War, which saw the end of sharecropping and farming-out as predominant systems of production due to the slump in the sugar and cotton markets and the selling out of plantations to local speculators who then divided these estates and sold to small holders for the wealth which the latter were able to accumulate during the wartime prosperity and high wages. Opportunities for emigration were reduced; Nevisian males stayed at home on their small plots and cultivated subsistence crops, some sugar cane, and some cotton for whatever price they were able to receive. Household labour predominated, pitchfork and hoe were still used. The government bought defunct estates and initiated expanded land settlement schemes in order to encourage the development of a yeomanry. The immediate post-war period of Nevis was the season of peasantry, both in modes and means of production.

After 1955 opportunities for emigration opened up again, not only to England, but to the U.S. Virgin Islands, where the tourist industry had begun to flower and, with it, demands for labourers in construction and the service occupations multiplied. And, as the cotton market rose for a short time and subsequently went into a steady decline, Nevisian labouring class households were again dependent upon cash remittances sent by emigrants, this time both male and female, while desultory cultivation of cotton and subsistence crops was carried on by the grandmothers, grandfathers and youngsters left behind. In 1962, more than 70 per cent of the adult population was not cultivating at all, save for a garden plot of yams, sweet potatoes, and garden vegetables on freehold and leasehold land. In the same year well over $600,000 BWI in postal and money orders were cashed, an amount greater than the proceeds cotton growers received during their biggest crop year since 1942. As I have stated elsewhere, remittances replace agricultural production as the main and most important source of wealth, by a wide margin.[13]

Accompanying this trend towards agricultural non-production and the increasing influx of wealth is the increasing availability of land. Estates are purchased, divided and resold in small parcels to foreign speculators in the tourist business as well as to Nevisians. To the latter, it would appear, land is considered more as a commodity rather than as capital for further productive use. Land is an investment, not only insuring social prestige, but economic independence, in the way of ensuring bank loans for further emigration. In this present period of Nevisian social and economic history, the means of peasant production are present, but are not used; the source of wealth is the cash wages of emigrant labourers. The cash is often invested in land, in shops, in cars and other consumer goods. Today in Nevis there is a curious mixture of dependence upon proletarian-like relationships, peasant-like holdings, and bourgeois aspirations and consumer behaviour. In any event, theirs is a marginal economy, and since there is now some question about whether they can continue to send emigrants abroad — to say nothing of the ability of the emigrants to continue to send remittances — they will be forced to seek out any means of making a livelihood by their own labour, whether for themselves or for others.

In the foregoing pages I have tried to point out that the development of seemingly disparate means and relations of production is possible, especially within the context of marginal, and perhaps only capitalist, economies. In the specific case of Nevis, a former British Caribbean colony, my argument has not been with the *concepts* of peasantry or proletarian *per se*, but with the categorical use of such concepts, since certain forms of production, e.g., sharecropping, may yield proletarian-like relationships in association with peasant-

[13]R. Frucht *Ibid.;* see also R. Manners, "Remittances and the Unit of Analysis in Anthropological Research," *Southwestern Journal of Anthropology* 21:3:179-195, 1965.

like techniques. In a different context this argument has been already made. Sidney Mintz suggests three historical contexts for the development of Caribbean peasantries: the early yeomen cultivators; a " 'proto-peasantry' which evolved under slavery," i.e., slaves who were allowed to cultivate and market food crops, and peasantries which developed in opposition to the slave plantation, e.g., Bush Negroes and Maroons.[14] There is some evidence that a "proto-peasantry" developed in the Leeward Islands and especially on Nevis,[15] but it did not become a "reconstituted peasantry"[16] after emancipation as in Jamaica. The small size of the Leeward Islands and the lack of open areas into which they could go forced the freed slaves/"proto-peasants" into wage labour and sharecropping relations. In terms of the means of production they remained "proto-peasants". Peasant-like production and marketing in these situations may be interpreted as the means by which planters reduced their costs of production by having the slaves provide for themselves, and later, under sharecropping, as the means by which plantation production was carried on in the face of cash shortage. In terms of the relations of production and the social division of labour, the slaves remain slaves, and the sharecroppers remain proletarian.

Furthermore, I am not arguing that Nevisian society is wholly proletarian (though because of its historic tradition and its pattern of labour migration a strong argument could be made for this case), but that the increasing wealth and rising standard of living invites thinking of the present day situation in terms of a *petit bourgeois* style of life. Such circumstances make it difficult categorically to apply terms like "peasant" or "proletarian". The special conditions noted here have to be taken into account, for instance, if attempts are made to organize Nevisian sentiment into political action. The rise of new, non-or anti-Labour Government political parties might be expected under these conditions.

Finally, comparisons of these materials for Nevis with those for other islands such as Montserrat, or even other areas, such as the lower Danubian basin described by Doreen Warriner,[17] may enable us to stipulate other sociological and ideological components accompanying the apparent disparities between peasant-like means of production and proletarian-like relations of production. One possible implication of such an attempt is that we will have to shift our attention from peasant and proletarian *community*, and describe and analyze peasant and proletarian *relations* in all their variety. This is to reiterate the point that peasantry and proletariat can be conceived of as both class *and* culture.[18]

[14]Sidney Mintz, The Question of Caribbean Peasantries: A Comment, *Caribbean Studies* 1:31-34, 1961, especially page 34.

[15]See, for instance, Elsa Goveia, *Slave Society in the British Leeward Islands at the End of the Eighteenth Century*, Yale University Press, New Haven, 1965.

[16]Sidney Mintz, Foreword to R. Guerra y Sanchez, *op. cit.*, p. xx.

[17]D. Warriner, *The Economics of Peasant Farming*, Oxford University Press, 1939.

[18]Sidney Mintz, The Folk-Urban Continuum and the Rural Proletarian Community, *op. cit.*, especially page 141; T. Shanin, *op. cit.*, especially page 17; Eric Wolf, *op. cit.*, especially pages 91-92.

JAMAICA TODAY

YAEL LOTAN

IMAGINE A MAN WHO, for as long as he could remember, has been a janitor of a building, as his father and grandfather had been before him. Living in the building and tending it caused him to identify with it to some extent, but when the day came and he was told that he would inherit the property, he could not immediately think of it as his own. Probably his first reaction would be to try and sell it to the highest bidder.

This is a rather brutal oversimplification of the psychology of the Jamaican today, shortly after independence. But it does bear a closer examination if one is to understand what is happening to the lovely island that has always been associated with the sweetness of rum and sugar and bananas and fashionable vacations. There is a relationship between the migrant itch of Jamaicans—who at all levels seem to want to go *somewhere else,* be it the United States, Canada, Britain or Africa—and the fact that our island today is being negotiated much like a piece of real estate. This stems largely from a weak sense of ownership and a confused sense of identity. There is no denying that economic factors help to bring about these phenomena, but the very same factors have not produced parallel results in other countries. We have not witnessed mass migrations from most of Latin America (Puerto Rico is a special case), nor the tendency on the part of properly elected native authorities to offer their countries to outsiders at a cut rate, believing this to be the only hope for survival. But then, the Latin Americans had to win their independence from Spain and Portugal by force, and since then have not doubted their national identities. It has been the peculiar fate of the British West Indies —populated largely with slave and bond importees—that independence failed to mean very much, in terms of dynamics, at the time it came. It is at present largely a symbolic matter, along with its trappings of flag, anthem, insignia and a diplomatic corps.

Yael Lotan is the daughter of the former Israeli Consul General to the U.S. She now makes her home in Kingston, Jamaica.

FREEDOMWAYS, Third Quarter, 1964, pp. 370-374.

Culturally, we are faced with an odd situation. The middle class, regardless of complexion, is still deeply involved with England in a peculiarly stultifying way. Despite the growing reaction, the attitudes of "black Englishmen" are still strongly prevalent among the civil servants, the small bourgeoisie, the school teachers and the like. It is less marked among the professionals, who have often been exposed to the United States and look to it as a spiritual home, however superficially. At the other end of the social scale are the various kinds of "Rastafarians," so called after the Emperor of Ethiopia, who ardently deny their connection with any place other than Africa, specifically Ethiopia, and mistrust any attempt to make a rational effort on their behalf. In between rest many amorphous groups whose identification is Jamaican almost, as it were, by default. This of course leaves out the relatively small communities who are identifiably Syrian, Chinese or East Indian, and whose connections appear ambiguous to an outsider. In the circumstances it is not surprising that a sense of *national purpose*, which must spring from national solidarity, is yet to find a form.

On the economic level the trend is towards a mass take-over by the corporations of the United States and a few European affiliates. The vacuum left by the stagnation of the sugar-citrus-banana-rum economy, is being rapidly filled by the commercial and industrial forces of North America. To start with, Jamaica's main value lies in her bauxite, of which she is the world's largest producer and without which there is no aluminum. (In 1962 Jamaica alone produced about seven and a half million tons of bauxite, or nearly one third of the world's total production of this ore during the Second World War.) This is being exploited by four major aluminum companies—Alcoa, Alcan, Reynolds and Kaiser. Their lease agreements enable them to take their profits out of the island in return for a royalty of approximately *twenty-eight cents* per ton of bauxite. Even this royalty and the insignificant tax levied on the companies is subject to reduction when the price of aluminum goes below a certain high mark. Thus, in 1963 the grand total of the Jamaican Government's revenue from the industry was a little over 15.5 million dollars. But Jamaica has other things to offer besides the yet unexploited possibilities of various raw materials and byproducts of the natural produce. Above all, the American businessman is attracted by the opportunity to save himself U.S. tax losses by operating even a nonprofitable enterprise outside. Combined with the tax holidays Jamaica offers him—now ranging from five to eight years—and the United States Government guarantee on such investments, the effect is almost irresistible.

In her anxiety to encourage these investments, Jamaica makes no attempt to arrange for eventual ownership of the enterprises, nor for local participation in them. The result is that almost the only benefit to the island is the employment these industries provide, and the wages are ridiculously low by U.S. standards, ranging officially from 21¢ to 34¢ per hour. (Compare with the U.S. *minimum* wage of $1.25 per hour.) The executive staff, by and large, is imported, at U.S.-level wages and more, plus many fringe benefits. A native Jamaican, however skilled or trained, finds it very hard to obtain the employment his training has equipped him for—outside the civil service—and even the few local business houses will often import a British or American at a premium rather than employ one of their own. Insurance companies, finance companies and banks are all, of course, British, American or Canadian. Thus while ostensibly the balance of trade improves, the nation's economic reality actually deteriorates.

Jamaica's ambassador to Washington described foreign investment as a 'shy little bird." This is astonishing, since the history of the Western Hemisphere has shown it to be something closely resembling a rapacious eagle. And it is the very same companies, e.g., "Grace" and United Fruit and Bookers—who are spreading like wildfire in Jamaica today. These interests, incidentally, maintain the local press through their advertising, with obvious results. Mercifully, Jamaica has no oil, although bauxite seems to be doing the job pretty well.' Even the most tightly controlled Latin American states have at least attempted to place a ceiling on the percentage of exported profits; Jamaica so far has not done so. A government corporation, by name of JIDC, is in charge of the "bargain-counter," offering our cheap labor, our political stability and lack of foreign exchange control (only to the outside investor, that is) and will actually build the plants for them on favorable lease-terms. Unfortunately, this has come to mean that the system develops a vested interest in maintaining labor cheap—and a margin of unemployment at all times, since full employment inevitably leads to increased wages—and perpetuates the absentee landlord in a new guise. At the same time a superficial impression of boom is created—and very useful it is in an island 90 miles from Cuba—through the cropping up of factories, office buildings, apartment houses and the like. Most food products—even the staples, such as rice and cornmeal and fish—are being imported (a vast proportion of it by "Grace") and their cost is far too high in relation to wages. The cost of living rises dizzily, wages barely creep up. The island has acquired a taste for consumer economy, and has done little to provide this trend with a truly sound economic basis. The attempts to cut importations and increase local production are, in the final analysis, meaningless if the inducement to do this is given to the foreign investors who export their profits. And the price of the goods hardly changes when they begin to be manufactured locally.

The result is that behind the facade of boom misery increases daily, slums around Kingston are growing faster than they can be cleared by the impoverished government, slums which are created by the misleading demand for industrial labor and by the stagnation of agriculture. There is a danger that Jamaica will end up as a second-rate Hong-Kong.

How is one to understand this development? Is the government, duly elected by the people in decent two-party elections, actually anxious to sell the country to outside interests? Is the absence of restrictions on the exportation of profits or economic control, a symptom of corruption? I doubt it. If there is corruption, it is small and insignificant on the whole. No, the reasons seem much more fundamental and therefore more discouraging: the still-uncertain understanding of true sovereignty; inexperience and too great a respect for American capital and "know-how"; an inadequate knowledge of Latin America; and finally, a political system which rests on two parties all too close in their ideologies (headed by two cousins) and run by the same middle-class, foreign-educated sector of the public. Even more disastrously, each party has its affiliated trade union organization which it uses in all the obvious ways as a weapon in the partisan political campaign. The unions represent but a fraction of the working class—mostly the white-collar or near-white-collar workers. The great mass of unemployed or casually employed is really out of the picture. To the poor Jamaican today it is *"plus ça change, plus c'est la même chose"* or "six of one and half-a-dozen of the other." Unless there is a change within the parties themselves, we might just as well adopt the Colombian gimmick of rotating the two parties in power.

A tragi-comic instance of Jamaica's mood was the issuance of a postage stamp with the picture of the winner of a commercial beauty contest in England—it was the first time that a Jamaican person was given such an honor.

Most of our writers and intellectuals are still in England—physically or spiritually. Most of our professionals, businessmen, politicians and go-getters are in the United States—physically or spiritually. The rest languish in near despair, afraid that beneath the fine talk about stability, progress, homeland and the rest, lies a sad truth that there is no real independence and hence a stagnant future. This cannot be cured by decree nor glossed over with good intentions. The change must come from within, when all the divers groups come to realize that their common stake is in making their home their own.